ST. PATRICK'S

The First 100 Years

By

William R. Hoover

Edited by Malinda R. Crumley and Kay Fialho

ISBN: 0-9621410-0-3

Page 4 photos:
Taken from The Bohemian, *Vol. 1, 1899-1900*
#4, Harvest Home Number, Page 84 and 90
(An early literary magazine published by the
Bohemian Society of Fort Worth).

CONTENTS

SWARTZ

SWARTZ

Prologue

By the year 1875, some order and regularity had come to the religious lives of the Catholics of Fort Worth. Mass was said on the last Sunday of each month at the residence of the Carrico family on Third and Rusk Streets. This scheduled service was occasionally augmented by the welcome visits of Father Claude Martiniere from Wylie, in Dallas County. Between them, Father Perrier and Father Martiniere had the spiritual care of the little flock well in hand. This had been the way of things in Fort Worth for some years.

Then came 1876, a year which brought great changes in the form of the assignment of the first resident priest and the construction of the first parish church. Early in 1876, Bishop Claude Dubuis of Galveston named Father Thomas Loughrey as the first resident pastor and authorized the building of a church which was to be dedicated to the Polish Jesuit, Saint Stanislaus Kostka.

Father Loughrey was born in Killaloe in the Irish midlands on June 10, 1848. Along with other members of his family he came to Texas to escape the famine conditions in his own country. The Galveston Ordination Book shows that he received tonsure and the minor orders from Bishop Dubuis in the Galveston cathedral in 1871, and that he was ordained subdeacon, deacon, and priest during the week of April 6 to April 13, 1873, in St. Mary's Cathedral by Dubuis. His first assignment was to Jefferson in far east Texas. He was then sent to nearby Marshall, where St. Joseph's Parish remembers him as its founder and first pastor. He was still a young man of 28 when he came to Fort Worth the beginning of summer, 1876.

He came fired with the determination to build. The first step was to secure property. In July, Daniel O'Flaherty, Joe Moore, and Thomas Carrico, acting for the diocese, purchased lots 4 and 5 with 100 feet of frontage on Throckmorton Street for $300. The original owner was E. M. Daggett, whose name is given to that whole addition. The lots were in the

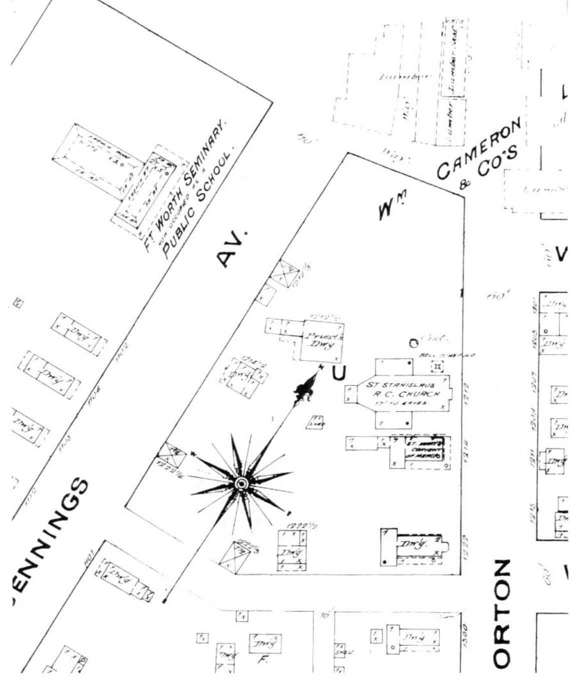

1200 block and thus were at some distance from the heart of town. That caused criticism. However, in a few years the growth of the city more than vindicated the choice of the site.

The Catholics of the city were enthusiastic and willing not only to give generously but also to work hard. A festival was held on September 21, 1876, to which the whole town was invited. It featured music, dancing, refreshments, and the raffle of "several handsome and ornamental objects." Mrs. Carrico, Mrs. Austin, and Mrs. Moore were the organizers of the event which was to benefit the new church.

St. Stanislaus Church was ready for use by the end of October, and the first High Mass was sung by Father Loughrey on Sunday, October 29, at 10:00 a.m. Henry Miller, who had a music store on the corner of Rusk and Weatherford, loaned the congregation an organ for the occasion. The pews were not yet installed, but they were on the way. The church was of modest size, 64 feet by 32 feet, with large sacristies on either side of the sanctuary.

Father Pierre Antoine Levy, who worked in the area in Father Loughrey's day.
Photo courtesy of Catholic Archives of Texas.

Father Claude Martiniere. In 1879 he was appointed to be the second pastor of St. Stanislaus. That appointment was rescinded and Father Loughrey remained until 1884.
Photo courtesy of Catholic Archives of Texas.

Seating capacity was 300. All this in only three months!

The geographical boundaries of the parish extended far beyond the limits of Tarrant County. Other priests occasionally assisted Father Loughrey in covering the territory. Among them was Father Pierre Antoine Levy, who ministered in the Johnson County area.

Father Loughrey was obviously well regarded in the community. In February of 1879 word came from Galveston that he was transferred to Dallas and that Father Claude Martiniere was named as pastor of St. Stanislaus. There was dismay over the news. *The Fort Worth Democrat* reported on February 23, 1879: "A petition has been signed by numerous business men and citizens praying the Rt. Rev. Bishop Dubuis of Galveston to allow Father Loughrey to continue as pastor of the Catholic church instead of sending him to Dallas, as has been contemplated." Apparently, the petition was heeded. Father Loughrey stayed on as pastor until 1884.

We have glimpses of parish life in the late 1870's. Father Loughrey taught school daily in the church building, drawing a curtain across the sanctuary during class hours. The City Directory says the school had 46 scholars in 1878. A priests' residence faced Jennings Avenue, behind the church and connected to the sanctuary. The church, of course, faced Throckmorton Street. It stood on approximately the same ground as the present rectory. Some of Father Loughrey's family also lived in Fort Worth, and there were Loughreys in the parish for three generations.

Other glimpses from the period tell of a Strawberry Festival in 1877 to raise funds for an organ, a collection made in 1879 for plague victims in Memphis, Tennessee, and a grand supper held that same year in Burt's Hall on Main Street. The supper featured a raffle and voting for the most popular young lady. Miss Haxel and Miss Alexander were the contestants, and Miss Alexander won. Mmes. Harris, Barlow, Dodd, Tackaberry, and Jemeson were in charge of the affair. Mrs. Moore and Mrs. Byrne presided over an "oyster table" in the center of the room. Admission to the supper was 25¢. The proceeds went to the poor of the city.

In December of 1879, the city council enacted a resolution allocating three acres in the new cemetery to the Catholics for their burials. *The Daily Democrat* thanked Mayor Beckham and the council for this action since, "as is well known, it is a rule of this church that all members who die in the faith are to be interred in consecrated ground."

Finally, in that era, the St. Stanislaus Sunday schedule offered a Low Mass at 7:30 a.m., High Mass at 10:30 a.m., and instruction in the catechism at 3:00 p.m.

****

Father Loughrey left St. Stanislaus in 1884, and his place was taken by Father Jean Marie Guyot. By 1885 plans were being made for the new church. It was to be called St. Patrick's. A lifelong parishioner, Vincent Duross, said in an interview that his father had told him that the name was changed as the result of a vote taken at a meeting of the parishioners. During the building of St. Patrick's, from 1888 to 1892, Fort Worth Catholics continued to worship in the old frame church, even as the massive stone walls were rising only a few feet to the north. In 1892 St. Stanislaus was abandoned as a church but continued in use as a parochial school for boys. It was staffed by the Sisters of St. Mary from St. Ignatius on the adjoining property. It had been partitioned into classrooms. As a school, the building survived for fifteen more years. In 1908 it was demolished to make room for the new rectory which was completed that same year.

Before beginning the story of *St. Patrick's: The First 100 Years*, we offer our gratitude and respect to St. Stanislaus and the faithful Catholics who made it all possible.

The Ancient Order of Hibernians assembled in front of the Roche house. St. Stanislaus Church is seen behind the ornate fence. *Photo courtesy of St. Patrick Cathedral Archives.*

CHAPTER 1

A Good Man Is Dead

ather Martiniere couldn't shake the thought from his mind. As he looked at the open, American faces of the priests in the sanctuary and the front pew, and out across the railing at the packed church and the casket of his friend, stately among the candles in the center aisle, the thought kept coming back. "This is a turning point. The old days are gone. Our Texas church has grown up. Guyot has gone to join the others, and I will follow soon."

The choir chanted on, the rhymed Latin phrases describing the judgment day:

Then before Him shall be placed
That whereon the verdict's based,
Book wherein each deed is traced.

"Well," thought Martiniere, "our deeds—mine, Guyot's and all the rest—belong to the century that has passed." His gaze moved up the stone columns to the high vaulted ceiling. "What a splendid church," he thought. "What a monument to Guyot, and how proud he was the day it was dedicated." He looked again at the crowded pews. "So many people now, and there were so few when we came to Texas." Recollecting himself, he tried to turn his attention back to the unfolding ritual. But the sense of history rested heavily on his mind. Father Martiniere couldn't shake the thought.

Small wonder that the past was on his mind, for he was Father Joseph Martiniere, and he was officiating at the funeral of Father Jean Marie Guyot in the absence of the Bishop. It was Tuesday, August 6, 1907, and both the officiant and the deceased had come from France to Texas as seminarians forty years before.

Martiniere, the elder of the two by seven years, had crossed the Atlantic in 1863 and had been ordained the following year in Federally occupied New Orleans by Galveston's Bishop

Claude Dubuis. Guyot, crossing after the war was over, had come directly to Galveston. Only twenty years old when he arrived, he received the minor orders and subdiaconate, but priesthood was delayed until 1870. Bishop Dubuis had ordained Guyot as well. Martiniere could recall the day. "Another age, another world," he thought.

"Laus tibi, Christe," came the response to the Gospel. By this time the crowded pews were a sea of flapping fans. It was drawing nigh to ten

o'clock, and the sun was high. Though the windows were open, there was no stir of breeze in the church. The assembled priests were mopping their brows, and Martiniere was briefly sorry for them—until he remembered that he was the only one still fasting. The servers presented the wine and water. As he recited the offertory prayers he heard the choir beseech St. Michael to bring the souls of the dead to the light which God had promised "to Abraham and to his seed forever." A hush fell on the church as the words of consecration were pronounced. The communion finished and the tabernacle closed, the Mass drew to its conclusion. It was time for Monsignor Blum to mount the pulpit for the traditional eulogy. The celebrant watched as the preacher climbed the pulpit steps. The old priest knew the speaker well. "Something of an old timer himself," he thought, for Father Joseph Blum had succeeded him as pastor of Dallas' old Sacred Heart Church on Bryan and Ervay streets. "That was in 1889," he mused. "That old church is gone now. Bishop Dunne wanted a first-class cathedral for Dallas, and he has it in the new Sacred Heart." He looked around the church again. "But Guyot was the one that showed the way. There was not a church like this in Texas, not even in Galveston, when he began to build. There were those who thought him overambitious when they heard his plans. I simply thought he was brave. Well, Blum admired Jean Marie, too. Let's hear what he will say about it."

The pastor of Sherman had admired Father Guyot, indeed, and his regard was evident in the words of the eulogy. Knowing that St. Patrick's had been Guyot's, and Guyot, St. Patrick's, he spoke the praise of the church as well as of the man. Father Martiniere nodded approval as the preacher recalled incident after incident of the dead man's life and called attention to the beauties of the church he had built. He would try to remember Blum's words so that he could repeat them to the absent Bishop when he returned to Dallas. On second thought, however, he had something more remarkable for the Bishop. Earlier that morning, the local priests had been discussing an editorial which appeared in the *Fort Worth Telegram.* Written by a staffer, it was the paper's tribute to Father Guyot. Its sincere simplicity had appealed to the priests. Martiniere thought that it would have appealed to the unassuming

Guyot, too, more than Blum's eloquent words. Knowing that the Bishop would like it, he had folded the page carefully and slipped it into his coat pocket. The editorial had read:

A Good Man Is Dead

There died at St. Joseph's Infirmary Saturday, Rev. Father John Guyot, sometime priest of St. Patrick's Church in Fort Worth, who spent nearly thirty years here building up a parish and living a simple, kindly life.

There are many people in Fort Worth who will sincerely mourn the death of Father Guyot, who were never inside his church and who would not know a litany from an *ave.* They will mourn him because he was a good citizen and one of the men who helped build up Fort Worth in ways other than selling municipal bonds, or persuading packing companies to build plants here.

Victor Hugo, who was writing in Paris his wonderful *Les Miserables* just a few years before Father Guyot was born near the same French capital, had occasion to tell something about the Bishop of D. ＿＿＿＿＿. He very wisely gave up at the outset trying to tell anything about the character of the bishop, but wrote instead a few chapters of incidents in the bishop's life, with the result that for nearly fifty years the Bishop of D. ＿＿ has been one of the finest characters ever portrayed in fiction. The life of Father Guyot might have been taken by Hugo for his model and to write about it best would be only to tell incidents gathered here and there from a period covering nearly a third of a century.

Father Guyot came here in the latter part of the '70's to begin a ministry that was ended only by his death. He had saved a little money and if he had invested it in Main Street lots, he might have died rich. Instead he used the money to found a church, which is one of the notable edifices in Fort Worth. He lived on less than $10 a month and took no salary from his humble parish for many years.

Apparently his poverty was never considered by him. He simply forgot about it and went on with his work. When the church was building people would sometimes go there and inquire of a humble workman where they might find "the father."

"I will go and tell him," the man would answer with a smile and then he would go into his house, change his clothing, and come back to discuss the affairs of his church.

During the nearly thirty years he lived here, many other ministers of many other creeds have come and gone. There have been men famous as revivalists whose work added great numbers to their congregations. There have been others known as "church builders" to whom structures of brick and stone stand as monuments. Others have been known for their oratorical ability or their learning, and their names have appeared in print always followed by letters of title from divinity schools.

Jean Guyot was "Father" Guyot when he came to Fort Worth, and he remained "Father" to the end. His unassuming, continuous service as a priest in the same parish for so long a time is an eloquent tribute to the mighty simplicity of the church he represented.

To most men of similar service in later years would have come the dignity of long service, position and influence. Father Guyot died as plainly as he had lived. Throughout his life he ministered to the spiritually sick, and death found him in a hospital among the sick in body.

Fort Worth is better for having furnished room for such a life.

****

The eulogy was over, and Father Martiniere rose for the prayers of the absolution. "Enter not into judgment with Thy servant, Lord, for in Thy sight no man shall be justified unless remission . . . be granted." The old priest looked at the oaken casket before him and thought, "Guyot suffered enough for his sins, such as they might have been. He hadn't really been well since his operation in Chicago two years ago. Well, I'll pray for him, for me, and for all of us. May the angels take us to Paradise."

The procession moved toward the massive main doors, the casket having been turned. Father Martiniere followed closely after the altar boys who carried the candles and held the crucifix aloft. Having reached the entrance, he stood aside to watch the exit of the other participants. The honorary pallbearers came first. Father Martiniere didn't know their names, but they were George Laneri, Walter Daughterty, Eugene Roche, Jere Roche, J. J. Whelan, Frank McGhee, and Martin Lavin. They were followed immediately by the working bearers: John F. Lehane, D. H. Kernaghan, W. R. Mignon, J. D. O'Reilly, E. C. Orrick, Edward Finn, and John Moore. "Pillars of parish and community, all of them," Martiniere was sure.

He was glad that the priests were so well represented. These he knew and mentally ticked off their names as they went out the door. "Blum, of course, then Hayes, O'Connor, Harrington, and Finney, all of Dallas; Granger and Thion from Marshall; Nolan of Gainesville; McGinn of Denison. There's Father Mulloy from All Saints in North Fort Worth; McKeough from Cleburne; Schauf from Abilene; Donohue from Tyler; Byrne from Waxahachie. There's J. L. Harrington from Oak Cliff; Millinger of Pilot Point; Cusick of Brownwood; Kelly from Clarksville; Vernimont of Denton; Murphy from Wylie; and Haas from Alma. Here come Goessens from Henrietta and Ptanski from Ennis. Father Baker from Thurber is last except for the two friends from Louisiana, Father Trainor of Franklin and Father Jouan of New Iberia. So many of them! How gratifying!"

After the clergy came the sisters; those of St. Mary of Namur, the entire community, then Sisters of Charity of the Incarnate Word, all that could be spared from the infirmary where Guyot himself had received their care only a few days before.

As Father Martiniere went out the main door, he was astonished at the crowds and at the large number of vehicles lining the streets, almost a hundred, he would be told later, a cortege more than twelve blocks long. Seated beside Blum in the carriage, he looked around. There was St. Ignatius, very imposing; there old St. Stanislaus, dwarfed by its proud stone neighbors and long since partitioned into classrooms. Beyond, down Throckmorton Street, he could see the warehouses along the railroad—that railroad which had drawn the old town southward like a magnet. He remembered that the area had almost been open country when the parish began to build. Now it was all engulfed by the growing city.

As the carriage lurched to a start, he took a last look at the facade of the church. "The building will always be a reminder of Guyot," he thought, "his real memorial no matter what they put over his grave at Calvary." Briefly he wondered if the spires which the dead man had planned would ever be added to the flattened towers. "Maybe his successor will do it, whoever that might be."

The procession moved up Throckmorton past the City Hall and turned right toward Houston.

The funeral procession moved north on Throckmorton Street from the entrance of the church. That scene in 1899 and in 1988.
Photos courtesy of Mack and Madeline Williams, and St. Patrick Cathedral/David Barros photographer.

become a Jesuit and had even gone to Rome seeking permission to do so. They remembered the distress of Bishop Dubuis who had misinterpreted the purpose of Guyot's trip and the coolness that had developed between the missionary bishop and the quiet but determined Guyot. "A lot of water under the bridge," they said, referring to the passage of time rather than to the muddy trickle of the Trinity flowing beneath them in the 93-degree August sun. As they turned off North Main, approaching the cemeteries, they remarked how the area was building up with new structures lining the street as far north as they could see. "A parish and a school of their own over here now," said Blum.

At last they came to the gate of Calvary Cemetery, given to the Catholic people by the city many years before. They waited there in the sun as the rest of the long procession drove through the gate. Father Martiniere knew that before the bridge was built the bodies of the dead had been ferried across to the cemetery from the city on the other side of the river. By now hungry and tired, Father thought of the dinner awaiting them at the Knights of Columbus Hall and of the rail trip back to Dallas that lay ahead of him.

The service at the grave was mercifully brief. The last sprinkling and incensation were soon done, and the casket was lowered into the waiting steel receptacle in the ground. Martiniere turned to the crowd around him, spoke a word of thanks and dismissal, and returned to the waiting carriage. His foot on the running board, he turned again to the still open grave for a last prayer for his friend. "May his soul find its way to God and his body rest peacefully here until Judgment Day," he said.

Who can doubt that the first part of his prayer was heard and that the soul of the gentle priest was with God? But the second part of the prayer did not come true. Forty-one years and three months later the body of Jean Marie Guyot, disinterred, in other hands, was to retrace the route of that last journey. It was to be brought back to his beloved St. Patrick's and reburied under the high altar of the church— the church which was the fruit of his vision, the achievement of his life, and the child of his faith.

There they could see the excavation and foundation of Fort Worth's new skyscraper, modeled after the Flatiron Building in New York and scheduled for completion next year. Two more blocks, and they turned left on Rusk Street (one day to be known as Commerce). Moving north, the cortege passed through the busy commercial heart of the city. The two priests were pleased at the uncovered heads and other marks of respect paid to the passing hearse. The whole town knew who was being buried that day. On they went, past the corner of Third Street, where once had stood the Carrico family house, in which Father Perrier and other circuit riding priests had said Mass for a handful of Catholics thirty-five years before.

As they rounded the Court House, Fort Worth's pride, and began the descent to the Trinity River bridge, the two priests were again reminiscing about their departed friend. They recalled that he had once been determined to

GUYOT

One of Father Guyot's assistants went to see him in the hospital shortly before he died. He asked him for some of the specifics of his life and ministry, with a view to the historical value of the information. Father Guyot would only say: "Tell them I came here thirty years ago and have been here ever since." It was not much help to an historian writing eight decades later.

This writer wishes it were possible to give accurate information about the place and the date of the birth of Jean Marie Guyot, but our own research has been hampered by inaccurate information and the guesswork of others over the past century. I have no intention of compounding the confusion by stating as fact things that are really only conjecture. It often happens that something which is printed once is taken up by other writers and copied over and over again until repetition gives it the aura of truth. In 1950 Bishop Laurence Fitzsimon of Amarillo, a fine historian, and Monsignor J. G. O'Donohoe did considerable research on Father Guyot's origins. With the co-operation of church officials in Lyon, France, a search was done of the baptismal registers of Le Chambon-Feugerolles, Loire, and Tartare, Rhone, as well as Chandon and Cottances in the same region, without definitive results. The uncertainty is deepened by a challenge to Father Guyot's will after his death in 1907. Virtually everything ever discovered about his origin has been duplicated and is in the archives of St. Patrick's Cathedral, available to anyone interested in further research.

St. Patrick's Church in 1905. The crowd had gathered to welcome President Theodore Roosevelt, who visited Fort Worth that year. *Photo courtesy of Amon Carter Museum.*

A float in the 1900 Flower Parade. In the background are St. Patrick's Church, St. Ignatius School and the City Hall. The former priests' residence on Jennings Avenue may be seen behind the sacristy. *Photo courtesy of The University of Texas at Arlington Libraries.*

All existing clues fix the date of his birth in the period 1845-1848. As to the location, the clues all point to places in the Departments of Loire or Rhone, in France, just to the west of the great city of Lyon. Newspaper articles exist which say that he was born (a) near Paris, and (b) in Normandy, with no evidence offered for those places. His lifelong association with the Martinieres, Bishop Dubuis, and Father P. A. Levy, all from the Lyon area, point to that section of France as his birthplace.

It is possible to be more specific about his ordination to the priesthood. This took place at St. Mary's Cathedral in Galveston on December 17, 1870. The ordaining prelate was Bishop Claude Dubuis.

Catholic Directories still in existence make it possible to trace his career from ordination to his arrival in Fort Worth. In 1873 and 1874 he was in Liberty, Texas. The years 1875 to 1878 saw him attached to St. Mary's Cathedral in Galveston. The 1880 directory locates him at St. Patrick's Church in Galveston. In 1881 he is listed as vice president of St. Mary's University in Galveston (a small, struggling college of 150 students). In 1882 he was at Gainesville, Texas, with Father Levy; in 1883, at Denison, and in 1884, at Galveston once again, this time at the Ursuline Convent. The 1885 directory, of course, places him in Fort Worth in the company of Father T. K. Crowley.

When the Diocese of Dallas was established, Father Guyot was named a Diocesan Consultor and held that post until his death. In 1902, he was appointed *Defensor Matrimonii* for the diocese and continued in that function until his death.

His desire to join the Society of Jesus is a fact revealed in his own correspondence. In the spring of 1880, he went to Rome to seek the permission of Cardinal Simeoni of the Propaganda to become a Jesuit. The Cardinal persuaded him to return to Texas and, as he wrote to Bishop Dubuis, "for the reasons he gave me, I could not refuse." Dubuis himself was in Europe at the time, and Guyot tried to meet him at Charlieu in France to explain his trip. Dubuis was expected there but did not arrive. Guyot waited until August 23 and then returned to Texas. The Bishop's anger over his attempt was a source of great distress.

All recollections picture Father Guyot as a man of great simplicity and humility, always deeply affected by any kindness shown to him. He raised large sums of money but spent little on himself. His dwelling was a frame house facing Jennings Avenue just behind the site of the present rectory. There was a well in the yard enclosed by a wooden fence. Rusty drinking cups hung on nails on the fence. His yard was graced with magnolia and pear trees. He kept an owl as a pet. He enjoyed the services of one Patsy Haggerty, who was described as his "right hand man."

Father Guyot was ill for some years before his death. In 1905 he made a trip to Chicgo to submit to surgery there. He recovered from the operation, but it was the precursor of his death. He was admitted to St. Joseph's Infirmary some weeks before he died. He stoutly maintained that he would get better, although medical personnel held out no hopes for his recovery. He sank into unconsciousness at around 10:00 a.m. on Saturday, August 3, 1907, and died shortly afterward.

Guyot's Last Will and Testament was executed by D. H. Kernaghan. His estate came to about $11,000, of which almost $7,000 consisted of notes payable to him. Beneficiaries of the will were L. H. Hindsman of Fort Worth, Father W. F. Park of Fort Worth, Father J. Martiniere of Dallas, (Bishop) E. J. Dunne, and Mrs. Pierre Levy of Cottance, Loire, France. The priests remembered in the will were requested to "Say Masses for my intention."

A snowstorm in November, 1892, is the setting for this view of the outer wall of the sanctuary. The church was dedicated in July of that year.
Photo courtesy of Mack and Madeline Williams.

Father Guyot about the time he came to Fort Worth.
Photo courtesy of Catholic Archives of Texas.

Father J. M. Guyot taken in the early years of his pastorate in Fort Worth.
Photo courtesy of St. Patrick Cathedral Archives.

Father T. K. Crowley. Father Crowley worked in Fort Worth in the 1880's.
Photo courtesy of Catholic Archives of Texas.

Father Thomas Blakeney. An old source calls him "the first assistant St. Patrick's ever had."
Photo courtesy of Catholic Archives of Texas.

Father Thomas T. Coyne. He served at St. Patrick's in Father Guyot's time.
Photo courtesy of Catholic Archives of Texas.

Father J. M. Byrne. He served in Fort Worth in the opening years of the twentieth century.
Photo courtesy of Catholic Archives of Texas.

Students of St. Stanislaus Parochial School for Boys pictured at the church entrance with Father Guyot and two unidentified priests. The photo was lent by Susie Murrin Pritchett. Her father, Stephen Murrin, is the blond boy standing on the first step, sixth from the left.
Photo courtesy of Mrs. Susan Murrin Pritchett.

The Church in Texas which Father Guyot served so faithfully and the city of which he was a proud citizen were approximately the same age. Even though Catholicism had been present in Texas since the sixteenth century and had flourished for a while in the mission-building era of the 1700's, the Catholic Church as we know it in Texas had to make a new beginning in the 1840's. The missions had been abandoned, and the work of evangelization had ceased with the withdrawal of Spain from the region and the emergence of Mexico as an independent nation. The re-founders of the Catholic Church in Texas were Frenchmen who came here from their native country by way of New Orleans.

Foremost among them was the Vincentian, Father John Timon, who came to Texas in 1838. Father Timon traveled extensively in the young and insecure republic and came to recognize not only the problems but also the opportunities for the rebuilding of Catholicism in the region. He was instrumental in introducing Father John Mary Odin to Texas. Father Timon eventually surrendered the leadership of the missionary enterprise to Father Odin and returned to his own work in Missouri. Father Odin proceeded with determination and energy. The efforts of the two men were crowned by the establishment of an independent vicariate and then by the founding of the Diocese of Galveston. The date of this significant event was May 4, 1847.

At the time, the site of Fort Worth was only part of a vast, rolling prairie with herds of buffalo as well as deer, antelope and other wildlife in abundance. This land of plenty had been inhabited forever, it seemed, by Indian tribes which lived off its bounty, loved it, and naturally resented the intrusion of the whites. The intrusion, however, could not be stopped. On May 4, 1841, a militia company of 69 men commanded by General Edward Tarrant and his aide, Captain John B. Denton, attacked and defeated a large number of Indians at Village Creek, forcing them to abandon their camps and flee from what is now the eastern part of Tarrant County. The way was open for the white settlers. Three years later, at Bird's Fort, near present day Birdville, representatives of President Sam Houston and ten different Indian tribes signed a treaty dividing the settlements from the Indians' territory along a line which ran through today's Fort Worth, to Comanche Peak, then to San Saba and beyond to the Rio Grande. Thus, for a while, East was divided from West in Texas. The line of settlement was drawn, but a show of force was necessary to hold it. So, four years after the treaty and Texas' annexation to the United States, Major Ripley Arnold of the United States Army came to camp on a bluff overlooking a fork of the Trinity River. It was a defensible spot, so he made a permanent camp there, giving it the name "Camp Worth" in honor of General William Jenkins Worth, a Mexican War hero who had authorized Arnold's expedition. The date was June 6, 1849.

As Bishop Odin laid his plans for the new diocese, his thoughts did not extend that far to the northwest where the new military post overlooked the Trinity. His flock at that time was located in the regions nearer the coast and in the southern part of the state. There were ten permanent Catholic churches then, located at Galveston, Houston, San Antonio, Refugio, Castroville, Brown's Settlement in the Valley, Fagan's Settlement near Refugio, Santa Gertrudis, and Cummin's Creek in Austin County. In addition, there were eleven localities called Mass stations receiving regular or occasional priestly visits. The station nearest the new Camp Worth was at Nacogdoches, in far east Texas. When Camp Worth was established, there

Some of the priests who served in Texas in the mid nineteenth century. *Photo courtesy of Catholic Archives of Texas.*

CHAPTER 2

The Church and the City

were already 350 people in Dallas and 50 souls at Bird's Fort, perhaps Catholics among them, but as yet no visits from priests and no sacramental life. New towns were growing up, however, and there were Catholic soldiers in the garrisons of the military posts along the frontier. Eventually, the Bishop would have to give his attention to their religious needs; but in the early days of the diocese there were only ten priests to serve it. There were five others who had volunteered and were learning English, and only three seminarians.

The laborers were few, but money was even scarcer, if that was possible. Bishop Odin could expect little help from New Orleans or even from the Church in the rest of the United States. It was to his native France that he looked for help, and France responded with magnificent generosity. One of the most remarkable chapters in the history of the Catholic Church is the story of the incredible vitality and productivity of French Catholicism in the decades following the Revolution. The close of the eighteenth century saw the Church in France proscribed and persecuted, challenged by a rival establishment which the revolutionaries had set up, a constitutional church cut off from the ancient roots of the faith. But following the defeat of Napoleon early in the nineteenth century, Catholicism took on new life and energy. A sense of vocation arose in the land. Nourished by a deep piety centered around the devotion to the Sacred Heart of Jesus and the Immaculate Conception, the Church not only recaptured the soul of France but inspired an outpouring of missionary zeal and a commitment of resources to the apostolate such as has rarely been seen. The effect of this resurgence was felt in Asia, in Africa, and around the globe. Thus, the appeal of the early

leaders of the Church in Texas fell upon ears open to hear and hearts ready to give.

It would be impossible to overstate the value of the help given by the Society for the Propagation of the Faith, founded in Lyons in the year 1822, in the nick of time for Bishop Odin's appeal. Most of the religious orders which contributed to building up the Church in the state were either products or beneficiaries of this renewal. There were first of all Vincentians and Ursulines, older orders, but very much a part of the explosion of missionary zeal. Then came the Society of Mary, the Oblates of Mary Immaculate and the orders of sisters who did so much for Texas in the nineteenth century: Incarnate Word, Divine Providence, the Sisters of St. Mary, Belgian, but part of the same flowering, and many others who sent their missionary children to help build the Church in Texas a century ago. There were many individuals, too, who heard the appeal. Some were Irish, some German, some American, but most of the early ones were French, among them Jean Marie Guyot.

Meanwhile, back on the bluff overlooking the Trinity, the name of Camp Worth had been changed to Fort Worth, and in 1850 Major Arnold had moved his command into newly completed fortifications. They didn't stay long. The treaty notwithstanding, the Indians had been forced back to the north and west, and in 1853 Fort Worth was deactivated and the army detachment moved to Fort Belknap to the west. Only the name remained behind. Merchants and settlers moved into the abandoned fort buildings, and soon there was a small civilian population. In 1856 Fort Worth became the seat of Tarrant County, and by 1860 the population had increased to 450. The Civil War had a devastating effect on the little town. Many left to take part in the fighting. Indian raids began again with the army gone, and only a few farmers remained to till the soil. When the war was over in 1865, Confederate army veterans began to arrive, seeking to rebuild their lives and fortunes. They found abandoned homes and shops, a small half-completed courthouse, and a population of no more than 250. The only bright spot was that there were a lot of untamed, unbranded cattle roaming the frontiers of the state, and the war-depleted nation was hungry for beef. Fort Worth became a stopping place on the cattle trails and began to experience growth again.

In the ten years between 1866 and 1876, the population grew to 2,000. Between 1876 and 1877, from July to July, the population increase was fourfold, to 8,645. The reason was the coming of the railroads, the real builders of the West. The first Texas and Pacific train steamed into Fort Worth on July 20, 1876. The area between the bluff and the railroad some distance to the south quickly filled up with buildings and people. The new arrivals increased the Catholic population in an even greater proportion, for many of the railroad builders and maintainers, as well as the immigrants who followed the rails west, were Catholics—Irish mostly. Sincerely attached to their faith, they built churches and schools wherever they went. They found the faith already established in Fort Worth, but their numbers made some immediate changes necessary.

Indeed, before 1876 there had been neither a resident priest, nor a church. Missionary priests had visited the town from time to time in the late sixties as part of a circuit route that took them on horseback from Galveston, leaving in early spring, thence through the state as far as Henrietta. Passing through Fort Worth, they would say Mass in the courthouse, an available hall or a private home. There were only a handful of Catholics, but the priests' visits were undoubtedly very welcome. In 1870 a more systematic arrangement developed when Father Vincent Perrier, whose base was San Angelo, began visiting the town twice a year, spring and fall, apparently as part of a circuit that took him to various military posts. Many of the soldiers were Catholics. Father Perrier was important to them and they to him. In those Reconstruction days money was scarce. The soldiers were paid in gold, and what little money the priest ever had was given by them. In Fort Worth he said Mass at the homes of Colonel Griffin on Penn Street, Mr. Scott on Main Street, and at the home of the Carrico family which was a fine, large residence at the corner of Third and Rusk (now Commerce). A letter from Rose Carrico, a daughter-in-law of the priests' host, written many years later, says that her father-in-law, Thomas Ignatius Carrico, and his brother, Albert Basil Carrico, came to Fort Worth from Owensboro, Kentucky, in 1870. She wrote that two years later the wife of Thomas Ignatius and his three sons joined them. By an arrangement with Bishop Dubuis (who was a successor to Bishop Odin) priestly visits were increased. Father Perrier came once a month, and priestly service was augmented by periodic visits from Father Claude Martiniere who came from his post at Wylie (Dallas County).

This arrangement lasted through 1875. In 1876, because of the growth, Bishop Dubuis gave Fort Worth its first resident pastor. He was Father Thomas Loughrey. He faced a formidable challenge. The increased population made Mass in a home no longer feasible. A church was needed. In short order property was bought, and a church was built. Fort Worth's two newspapers, *The Daily Standard* and *The Daily Democrat*, reported that the first High Mass was sung in the new St. Stanislaus Church on Sunday, October 29, 1876. The *Standard* reported further that the church had been built in three months following the arrival of Father Loughrey in the city, "... a total stranger, without money and without a congregation, only a few Catholics being scattered here and there. The shepherd came and called his flock. They responded from the hills and vales, and were gathered together yesterday in their own fold."

A collage of photographs of the young men ordained in Galveston in 1871.
Photo courtesy of Catholic Archives of Texas.

H.W. WILLIAMS & CO. WHOLESALE DRUGGISTS
CLOTHIERS

CORNERSTONE AND DEDICATION

n midsummer of 1888, there were many signs of activity at the site of the Catholic Church on Throckmorton Street. The ground had been leveled, and each day under the hot Texas sun the teams of workmen were seen digging the carefully laid-out foundations. Deeper and deeper they dug, for the foundations were to bear a heavy weight of stone. Catholics watched the ongoing project with proprietary interest. It was their church. Months before, they had made the decision to build. Under the leadership of their pastor, Father J. M. Guyot, they had decided that the new church would not be a frame structure like St. Stanislaus, but a splendid creation of stone like the churches Father Guyot described from his boyhood memories of his native France. The people had

known that they would have to dig deep in their pockets as well, because the cost of the new building was estimated at $80,000, an awesome sum of money for a community of ordinary working people to raise. Many had seen the elaborate plans drawn by the architect, James J. Kane. All had seen the drawing of what the church would look like. Some were still grumbling about the expense, but most were dreaming of what the new church would mean to the religious lives of their families and to the prestige of Catholicism in Fort Worth.

By early October, the task of putting in the foundation was virtually complete. It was time to raise the walls and the towers. Much carefully cut native stone was already on the site. Before the actual

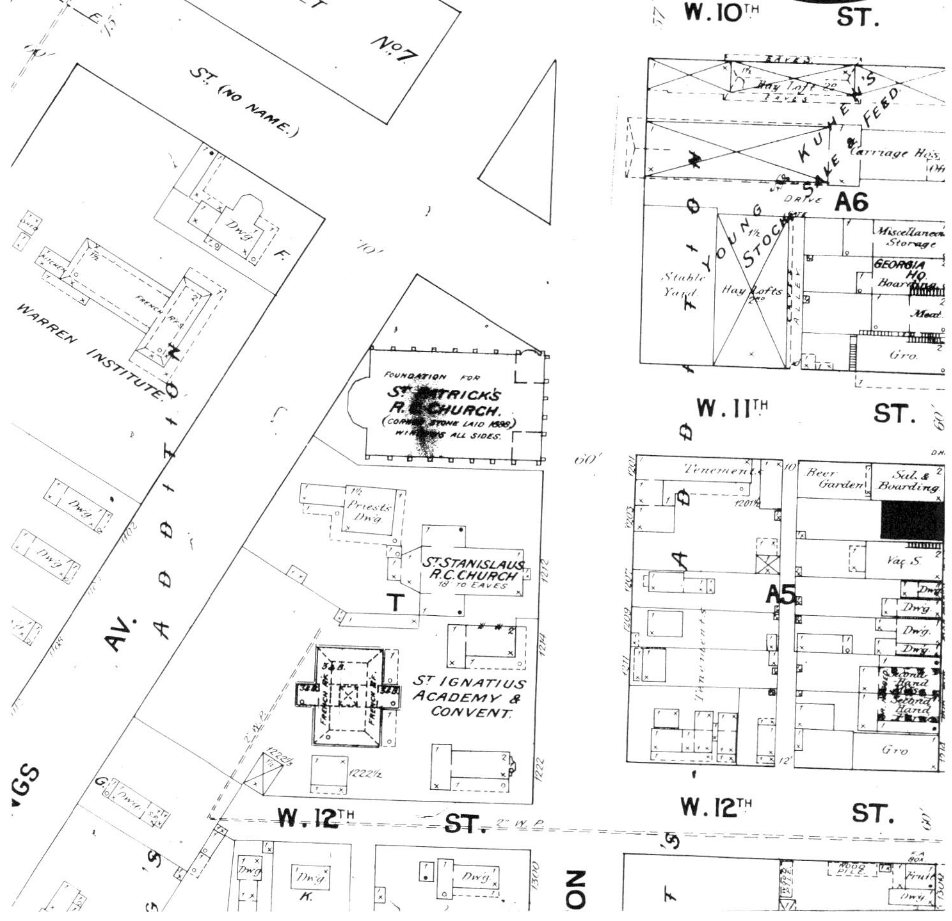

An 1889 map showing the site of the new church in relation to other buildings on the block.
Photo courtesy of Ruby Schmidt.

St. Patrick's Church under construction.
The photo was made in 1890 or 1891.
*Photo courtesy of St. Patrick Cathedral
Archives.*

construction began, it was necessary to dedicate the work by the blessing and laying of the cornerstone. A slab of limestone, hewn into a perfect quadrangular cubic shape, was at hand. It had been engraved on the three sides which would be visible. One side had been marked with a simple Latin cross. The opposite side bore the date "1888" and the name of J. J. Kane, architect. The side which would face the street showed the words "St. Patrick Church." The new church was to bear a new name, a matter of some pride to the Irish majority among the parishioners.

The Bishop of the diocese, the Rt. Rev. Nicholas Gallagher, a native of Ohio and Bishop of Galveston since 1882, came for the occasion, for it was a significant day for the diocese as well. The date chosen was Sunday, October 14. It was a full and busy day for all involved. The services began with a Solemn High Mass celebrated by Bishop Gallagher, assisted by Father Guyot and Father Flynn, a Jesuit, who was to be the preacher at the ceremony of the blessing. Visits from the Bishop were not too frequent in those days, and so Father Guyot presented a class of Confirmation candidates to the Bishop. They were confirmed at the end of Mass. Fifty-four young people received the sacrament.

The blessing of the cornerstone was scheduled for 4:00 p.m., and by that hour at least 800 people had gathered about the corner of the foundation. The Department band played a selection of sacred music, and then, according to the beautiful and solemn ritual of the Catholic Church, the stone was blessed and placed in position. The service was impressive. Father Flynn preached a beautiful and timely sermon which was listened to with attention by the multitude gathered around the stone.

****

The cornerstone of St. Patrick's Church. It was blessed on Sunday, October 14, 1888. *Photo courtesy of* The Texas Catholic.

Bishop Nicholas Gallagher of Galveston. He blessed the cornerstone in 1888. *Photo courtesy of St. Patrick Cathedral Archives.*

The church was almost four years in construction. Month by month, Catholics and their fellow citizens watched as course after course of stone was laid. They were heartened when the interior, pointed arches atop the granite columns were finished and the time came to put the roof in place. It was not easy to wait, but wait they did, for such construction is necessarily tedious and time-consuming, and most of the energy was supplied by human hands. Architect Kane lived up to his high reputation as he watched the building take shape, stone by stone. Father Guyot, likewise, worked on the building. Priests in those days had to have a great many skills at their command. All of them were

Bishop Thomas F. Brennan of Dallas. He presided at the dedication of the church, July 10, 1892.
Photo courtesy of Diocesan Archives, Diocese of Dallas.

builders and knew a great deal about mortar and stone. The newspapers of the time had predicted that the project would take years, for: "As is known, Catholics do not incur debt on their sacred edifices, deeming it improper to do so, and for this reason it sometimes takes years to complete a church." Be that as it may, the church was not completed until the summer of 1892, exactly four years after the job began with the excavation of the foundations. Halfway through the period Bishop Gallagher had returned to Fort Worth to confirm another class of forty-two girls and boys. That was on May 18, 1890. He observed the progress with satisfaction, but the responsibility was about to pass to another. In July of 1890, the Diocese of Dallas was formed, and to its new bishop fell the honor of dedicating the church.

****

The first Bishop of Dallas was the Rt. Rev. Thomas F. Brennan who came from Pennsylvania and became Bishop of Dallas in 1890. The dedication of St. Patrick's might well have been a bright spot in the eighteen unhappy months he spent in the diocese. At the time of the dedication, his tenure as bishop had only four months to run. Also presiding at the dedication was the Archbishop of New Orleans, the Most Rev. Francis Janssens. Janssens, born in Holland, had been a priest of the Diocese of Richmond, Virginia. He had served as Bishop of Natchez

Archbishop Francis Janssens of New Orleans. He assisted in the 1892 dedication ceremonies.
Photo courtesy of St. Patrick Cathedral Archives.

before becoming Archbishop in 1888. The Diocese of Dallas was part of the Province of New Orleans at the time. Not many priests came, for it was Sunday; but Father Crowley was there from Denison and Fathers Blum and Brinkley from Abilene. The Rev. Dr. Coffey gave the sermon.

The dedication was set for 10:00 a.m. that Sunday morning, July 10, 1892. By that hour the church was packed with people. Everyone wanted to witness the dedication and be present for the first Mass to be sung in the new church. The three altars were beautifully decorated with plants and flowers. The dedicatory ceremonies having been carried out by the two prelates, Father Guyot sang the first High Mass. The choir was magnificent. It consisted of: sopranos, Mrs. England and Mrs. Guy Price; alto, Miss Marie Bragassa; tenor, J. E. Shrob; basso, Professor Bayrhoffer; organist, Miss Ella Montgomery; flute, D. D. Lusk; and violin, Professor Kretlow. Father Coffey's sermon was much appreciated. He extolled the faith of the people and praised their sacrifices. He declared that the church was a symbol of the City of God and said that any city in America could be proud to have such an edifice.

This 1892 photograph is the earliest made of the interior of the newly completed church.
Photo courtesy of St. Patrick Cathedral Archives.

<u>LOG OF PROPERTY ACQUISITIONS</u>

<u>ST. PATRICK CATHEDRAL</u>

DATE PURCHASED	ADDITION	LOT #	BUYER	SELLER	PRICE
July 20, 1876	Blk T Daggetts	4 & 5	Bishop Dubois	E. M. Daggett	300.00
February 24, 1877	Blk T Daggetts	North 10 ft. of 3 All of 6	Bishop Dubois	E. M. Daggett	50.00
October 2, 1880	Blk 2 Jennings East	16 & 17	T. Loughrey	Thomas J. & Sarah G. Jennings	150.00
February 5, 1881	Blk 2 Jennings East	18	T. Loughrey	Thomas J. & Sarah G. Jennings	75.00
March 27, 1884	Blk 2 Jennings East	16, 17, & 18	T. K. Crowley	T. Loughrey	650.00
April 10, 1885	Blk 2 Jennings East	16, 17, & 18	Bishop Gallagher	T. K. Crowley	650.00
March 30, 1885	Blk 2 Jennings East	19, 20, & 21	J. M. Guyot	Sarah G. Jennings	900.00
February 17, 1888	Blk 2 Jennings East	19, 20, & 21	Bishop Gallagher	J. M. Guyot	800.00
May 25, 1881	Blk 2 Jennings East	North 15 ft. of 13 All of 14 & 15	T. Loughrey	Thomas J. & Sarah G. Jennings	112.50
July 7, 1887	Blk 2 Jennings East	North 15 ft. of 13 All of 14 & 15	St. Ignatius Academy	T. Loughrey	800.00
August 29, 1887	Blk 2 Jennings East	North 7-1/2 ft. of 14 All of 15	J. M. Guyot	St. Ignatius Academy	400.00
December 28, 1888	Blk 2 Jennings East	North 7-1/2 ft. of 14 All of 15	Bishop Gallagher	J. M. Guyot	400.00

<u>ST. IGNATIUS ACADEMY</u>

DATE PURCHASED	ADDITION	LOT #	BUYER	SELLER	PRICE
September 8, 1885	Blk T Daggetts	1 South 10 ft. of 2	St. Ignatius Academy	Jacob I. Smith (dwelling)	4,000.00
September 16, 1885	Blk T Daggetts	North 30 ft. of 2 South 40 ft. of 3	St. Ignatius Academy	Thomas Roche (dwelling)	4,000.00
	Blk 2 Jennings East	South 10 ft. of 13 All of 12 North 15 ft. of 11			
March 26, 1887	Blk 2 Jennings East	North 15 ft. of 7 All of 8 South 10 ft. of 9	St. Ignatius Academy	Sarah G. Jennings	800.00
July 7, 1887	Blk 2 Jennings East	North 15 ft. of 13 All of 14 & 15	St. Ignatius Academy	T. Loughrey	800.00
August 29, 1887	Blk 2 Jennings East	North 7-1/2 ft. of 14 All of 15	J. M. Guyot	St. Ignatius Academy	400.00
June 30, 1898	Blk 2 Jennings East	North 15 ft. of 9 All of 10 South 10 ft. of 11	St. Ignatius Academy	Hyde Jennings	1.00

CORNERSTONE AND DEDICATION

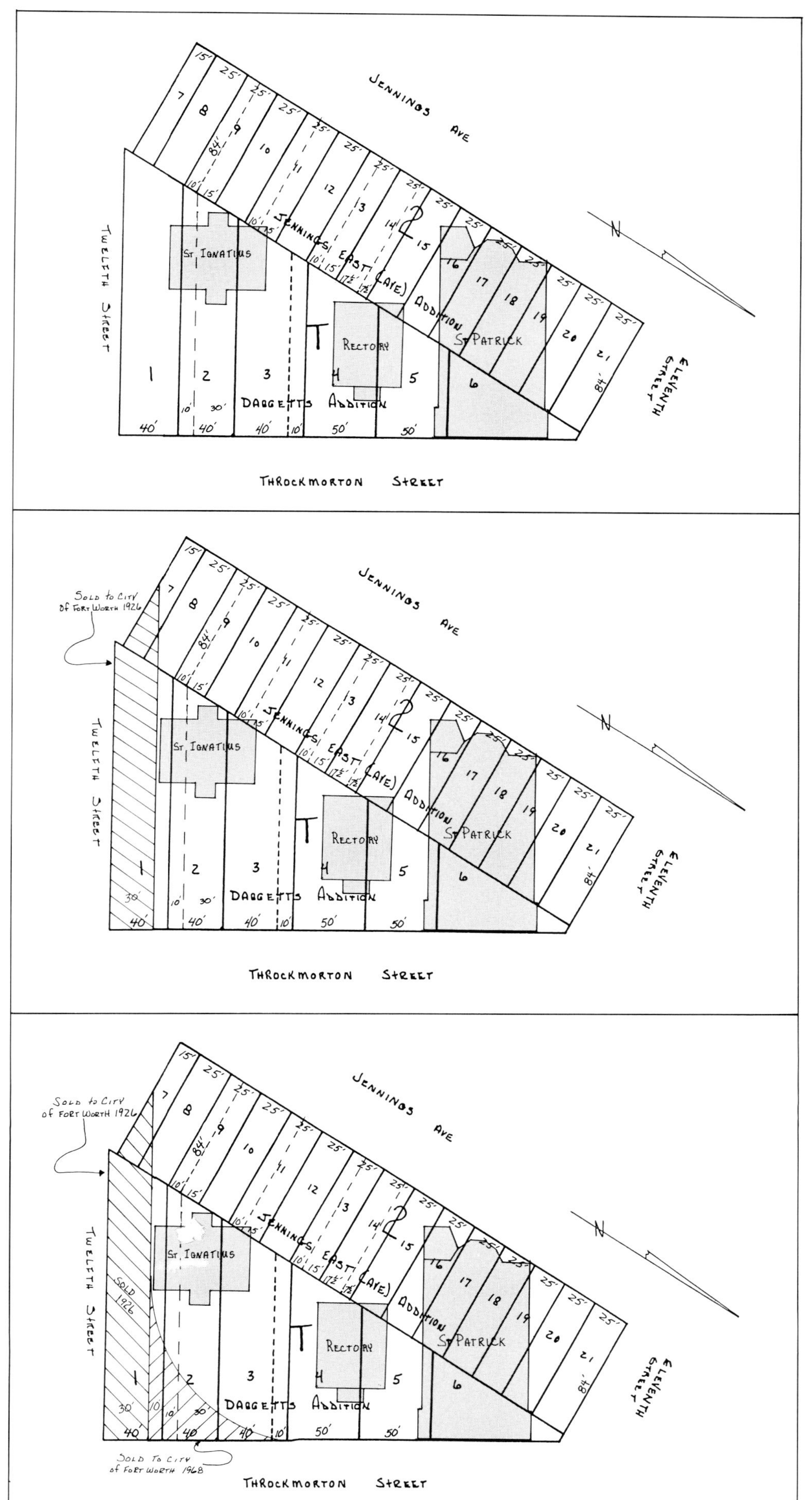

19 mm = 25'
.76 mm = 1'

0 10 20 30 40 50 mm

Maps drawn by
Vincent Fialho.

The pastorate of Father Robert M. Nolan spanned almost one-third of the one hundred years from the laying of the cornerstone of St. Patrick's Church to the present. When he became pastor of St. Patrick's in 1907, the city of Fort Worth had 68,115 inhabitants. Downtown Fort Worth had begun to take its present shape, although there were several hundred residences still standing and occupied in what is now strictly a business area. The residential sections of the city were growing to the south, east, west, and to the north, where the establishment of the meat packing plants had brought about a considerable growth in that almost autonomous section of the city. By 1907, Fort Worth boasted several busy railroads, and that very year the new Interurban line began regular service to Dallas. The local traction companies opened up new streetcar lines hand in hand with new residential developments.

The Catholic Church's presence in the city had grown, also. In addition to St. Patrick's Church and and St. Ignatius Academy, the city's Catholics were proud of the new All Saints Parish, which had been formed in 1902, and its companion institution, All Saints Academy. The academy, started in 1906, was soon replaced by Mount Carmel Academy. They were also happy about St. Joseph's Infirmary which had been opened in 1885 and had inaugurated a school of nursing in 1906. St. Joseph's was a fine facility, the key institution for health care in the area. It was well on its way to becoming, for a time, the largest Catholic hospital in Texas. A Knights of Columbus Council had been chartered in 1903. Its charter members were mostly St. Patrick's parishioners. Principal organizer of the council was Thomas P. Fenelon. Council 759—closely associated with St. Patrick's through the years—was, and remains, an asset to the Catholic life of the city. St. Patrick's itself enjoyed the services of several parish organizations. Notable among these was the choir which has rendered superb service since before the building of the church and is still a source of pride to the parishioners. The Altar Society, which was founded in 1883, has also served the parish since that date.

Such was the picture when Father Robert M. Nolan came from Gainesville to Fort Worth to assume direction of the parish. He was 33 years old and was described as an open, outgoing man, determined and even aggressive with a sense of humor and a tendency to look to the future rather than to the past. He needed those qualities because he had a difficult job to do.

The growth of the city had brought about a need for new parishes, and, in the first two years of Father Nolan's tenure at St. Patrick's, three were established.

The beginnings of Holy Name Parish can be traced to 1907 when the Sisters of St. Mary began teaching in a frame residence, called St. Ignatius Annex, on the southeast side of town. It

The clergy of the Diocese of Dallas on retreat in 1911. Bishop Joseph P. Lynch is seated (center). To his right is Monsignor Joseph Blum, who preached Father Guyot's funeral sermon. Priests associated with St. Patrick's are (1) Father Robert M. Nolan, (2) Father Vitus Graffeo, his assistant, and (3) Father Lido Parroccini, who ministered at St. Patrick's.
Photo courtesy of Catholic Archives of Texas.

CHAPTER 3

Old St. Patrick's

was the beginning of a new parochial school, and the sisters commuted by streetcar. The parish was formally begun the next year when a church was built on Terrell Street with Father Bernard Diamond as the first pastor. After a brief time, he was replaced by Father J. S. O'Connor who was pastor there for thirty-one years. Many of the early St. Patrick's parishioners transferred their loyalty to the new parish.

1908 also saw the beginning of St. Mary of the Assumption Parish due south of St. Patrick's in a fine residential section. A school was begun, and St. Mary's became a large and thriving parish. The Vincentian Fathers, at Bishop Dunne's invitation, provided the first pastor. He was Father Edward F. Park, and he supervised the construction of the first frame church on Magnolia and Jennings. It was destroyed by fire on August 31, 1922. Ground was broken almost immediately amid the ashes with Father Nolan giving the sermon for the occasion. The present handsome, Romanesque church was dedicated July 20, 1924.

Handley was not part of Fort Worth in 1907, but the new Interurban line made a stop there. The electric company had built a power plant and developed a recreational area called Lake Erie. It was a popular spot, and the population had grown. In 1909, St. Rita's Parish was established. The name was chosen by Bishop Dunne in honor of Rita, whose intercession, he believed, had cured a serious illness earlier in his life. Father P. J. F. O'Bierne was in charge. Priests from St. Patrick's provided the Sunday Masses in the early days.

Father Nolan began to make changes at St. Patrick's also. A new rectory was needed, for the days were gone when a single priest could meet the demands of the large parish. During Nolan's pastorate, there would generally be two, and sometimes three, priests besides the pastor in residence. In addition, Father Nolan's mother, Mrs. Margaret A. Nolan, resided at the rectory until her death; and his sister, Mrs. Mary Drake, lived there for nineteen years, serving as her brother's housekeeper.

Plans were drawn, and construction of the new rectory began in his first year. The house, which is still the rectory, was a large one with four big rooms upstairs, two with bay windows. There were two porches. A small one in front had a railing around it and at one time was partially roofed and screened. A larger one the width of the house was at the rear. Downstairs were six large rooms. In later years, much of the first floor would be used for offices, but Father Nolan had his bedroom and personal quarters there. Church offices were not common then, and much business was

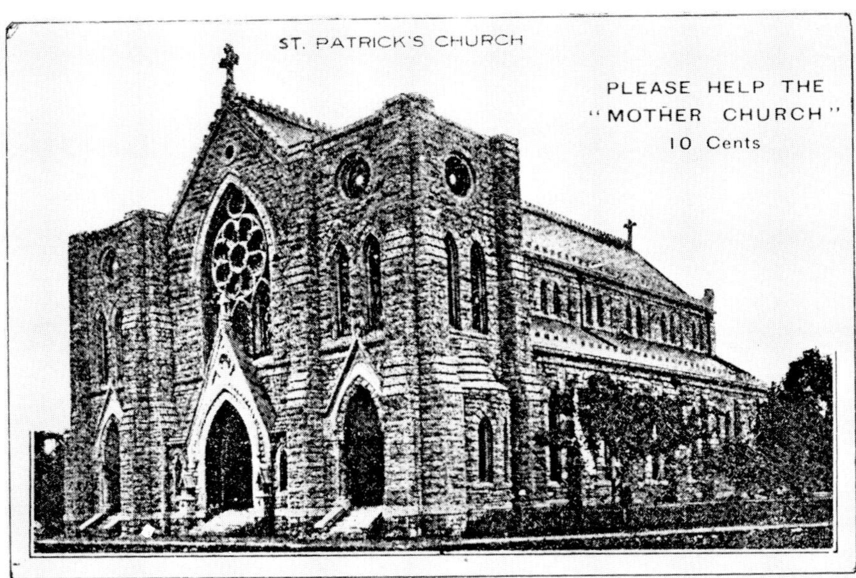

The cards were sold to provide for the church's needs.
Photo courtesy of St. Patrick Cathedral Archives.

transacted from the sacristy. Old-time parishiners tell of fireplaces and chimneys, but the traces of them are long gone. The basements, both of the rectory and the church, were excavated many years later. The house was much like other houses being built in Fort Worth at that same time.

All these things were costly, and the Catholics of Fort Worth were not affluent. Many of them were employees of the railroads or the packing plants and had little money to give. Old-time parishioners recall that the parish was quite hard up for funds, and that Father Nolan had to make appeals Sunday after Sunday for more contributions. No opportunity was overlooked to raise cash. Two senior parishioners, Misses Anna and Margaret Fenelon, were asked about their recollection of those difficult days. They recall that the children were taken out of school to sell cards, like postcards, on the street for ten cents each. Father Nolan was like many pastors of the time. The needs of churches and schools were great and pressing. Many fine priests, then and now, find that fund-raising has to be a major part of their activity. No one really liked it, but it had to be done. Though people might have complained that "Father is always talking about money," still they sustained their pastors in these efforts. In spite of the burden, churches continued to be built and embellished, and new schools were opened. There was a saying that to be in debt was healthy for a parish. Much of the sense of community that churches achieve comes from people and clergy facing adversity together.

St. Patrick's needed so many things, and Father Nolan was determined to provide them. The small Stations of the Cross were replaced with the present exquisitely beautiful ones. They are in the Gothic revival style and matched the original altars of the church. They

seem to have been a gift, at least in part, of John Laneri.

Another important addition was a pipe organ which Father Nolan was determined to have in place for 1913, the twenty-fifth anniversary of the laying of the cornerstone. The new organ was a Hook and Hastings tracker organ with 1,268 pipes. It was built under the supervision of R. J. Lamb who had been organist and choirmaster at St. Patrick's since 1895. A recital was held on July 11, 1913, which drew a record crowd. People sat on the chancel steps and stood in the church doors. Among those assisting Professor Lamb was W. J. Marsh, then organist at the First Presbyterian Church and later Lamb's successor at St. Patrick's. The event was a great success. Father Nolan addressed these words to the large crowd: "I consider your presence in our church a splendid demonstration of the friendship which St. Patrick's enjoys throughout the city."

It was wonderful, but it was hot. As a concession to the heat, the *Fort Worth Record* reported that "contrary to precedent in the Catholic Church, women will be admitted at the recital without headwear and gentlemen without coats."

A description of the growth of the Church during the pastorate of Father Nolan would not be complete without recounting the establishment in 1909 of Our Lady of Victory. In that year Father Nolan commissioned M. S. Sanguinet, a leading Fort Worth architect, to draw up plans for the new boarding school on 26 acres of land which the Sisters of St. Mary had acquired at the southern extremity of the city, at the end of the streetcar line at Hemphill and Shaw. The school grew in its early years, and in 1930 the sisters added a junior college and a novitiate at the facility.

Another significant event was the dedication of Laneri High School by Bishop Lynch on October 30, 1921. The school started with an enrollment of 67 boys distributed in grades five through nine. An additional grade was added each year until the high school was complete. The Brothers of the Sacred Heart staffed the school initially.

In 1961 these schools were merged into one high school for both boys and girls. That school was given the name of Robert M. Nolan.

Nolan was involved in everything that concerned the Catholic Church in Fort Worth,

Jennings Avenue, looking north from Lancaster in 1910. *Photo courtesy of Mack and Madeline Williams.*

The same view in 1930. *Photo courtesy of The University of Texas at Arlington Libraries.*

The same view in 1988. *Photo courtesy of St. Patrick Cathedral/David Barros photographer.*

for in 1913 he was appointed dean of the city and the surrounding area which included fourteen parishes as well as other institutions. It was a significant appointment for him and for the parish. Seemingly, the title of dean carried considerable weight in those days. Newspapers of the period and non-Catholics, generally, referred to him as "Dean Nolan." As dean he was the representative of the Bishop of Dallas. In 1910 a new bishop was appointed. He was the Rt. Rev. Joseph Patrick Lynch, and he served as bishop for an incredible forty-two years. He and Father Nolan were close friends, and he was a frequent visitor at St. Patrick's. Old-time parishioners remember him well. One of them, Herbert Manning, who was interviewed for this history, said: "Bishop Lynch was there quite often. He was a big man with bushy, white hair and a tremendous voice. I knew Bishop Lynch quite well, especially when I was working with the Knights of Columbus."

Manning went on to describe the parish celebration when Nolan became a monsignor. "The parish and the sisters decided that a collection should be taken up and given to Monsignor Nolan. They had a big celebration on Sunday night at church. The church was crowded. Louise Renfro and I walked down the aisle to the altar. I then turned and made a presentation speech that the sisters had prepared for me. Then Louise went over and gave him the burse with a bouquet of flowers." The year was 1925.

In the 1920's the relationship between the Catholic community and the community at large began to sour. The Ku Klux Klan became a powerful force in the life of the town. The organization had great economic and political clout, and Catholics were a target of their zeal. They professed a grand devotion to the purity of American ideals but, in fact, besmirched those ideals. The racist poison which was about to bear bitter fruit in Europe was not absent from American life. Catholics were not altogether guiltless of prejudice, but in this instance they were its victims. Catholics in Fort Worth found certain areas tightly closed against them. Employment was denied them by many prominent firms and even by agencies in the public sector. They also suffered acts of persecution. There were tar-and-featherings. The Grand Knight of the K. C. Council kept a baseball bat by his front door, and on one occasion had to use it. The Klan sometimes conducted downtown parades to show off its strength. On Friday, June 8, 1923, the Women's Auxiliary staged a parade twenty blocks long down Main to Twelfth Street and back up Houston Street to the Courthouse, thus passing within a block of St. Patrick's. 1,687 people marched. A plane flew overhead trailing a "fiery cross." The women bore banners with such slogans as: "We Stand for True Godliness, Purity and Loyalty," "Wives and Sweethearts of the KKK," and "One Hundred Percent Poll Tax Payers." There was anger and resentment among Catholics, but the experience had a good

effect on our people as well. As one historian observed: "Indifferent Catholics suddenly realized that they must fight for their faith—and fight they did. There was no such thing as carrying water on both shoulders as many had done in the past. At that time one was either a militant Catholic or on the other side."

In the twenties and thirties in spite of persecution in some quarters, the Catholic voice continued to be heard in the city. The newspapers carried Monsignor Nolan's sermons and reports of his doings, even his reviews of the motion pictures of the time. Clergymen of other denominations regularly appeared on speaking platforms with him. Such religious leaders as Rabbi Soskin of Temple Beth-El and Doctor Perry Gresham of University Christian, along with Nolan, hammered away at community prejudices and attempted to define a true Americanism for their befuddled fellow citizens. Rabbi Harry Merfeld and the Rev. L. D. Anderson of the First Christian Church spoke at a dinner at the Texas Hotel honoring Nolan on his twenty-fifth anniversary. Parishioners observed with astonishment that their pastor

Row 1: Father Peter Molloy, assistant from 1921 to 1928. To his right in row 1: Theda Scallon, unidentified girl, Dolly Allen, Mildred Manning, Beverly Petta, Frances Hammond, Ellen Welch, Monsignor Robert Nolan. Row 2: (l. to r.) Paul Droppleman, Mary Belle Glass, Mary Theresa Cough, Mary V. Hudgins, Louise Renfro, Rose Hammond, Anna Maria —. Row 3: (l. to r.) Billy Glenn, Charles Zlathovich. Row 4: (l. to r.) Jack Dacy, Elizabeth Coon, Marguerite Barnes, Dorothy A. Farrell, Martha Jane Farrell, Bonnie Mae Barnes. Row 5: (l. to r.) Bernard Haubert, Graham Keene, Herbert Manning, Robert Jones. Row 6: (l. to r.) Jareth Edwards, Allen Wagner, Rudolph Clements, Thomas Edwards, Vincent Kelleher. *Photo courtesy of Mrs. Eileen Farrell.*

Father Alphonse Bock was an assistant at St. Patrick's in the early 1920's.
Photo courtesy of Mrs. Lillian Ramsey.

Father Henry Felderhoff, assistant at St. Patrick's in the 1930's.
Photo courtesy of St. Patrick Cathedral Archives.

Father Clair McTamney, another assistant to Monsignor Nolan.
Photo courtesy of St. Patrick Cathedral Archives.

Father Ernest Langenhorst, assistant at St. Patrick's from 1930 to 1941. The couple are Guy Thompson and Kathleen Simon Thompson. The servers are Dan Simon, at Langenhorst's left, and Jim Jones.
Photo courtesy of Mr. and Mrs. Guy Thompson.

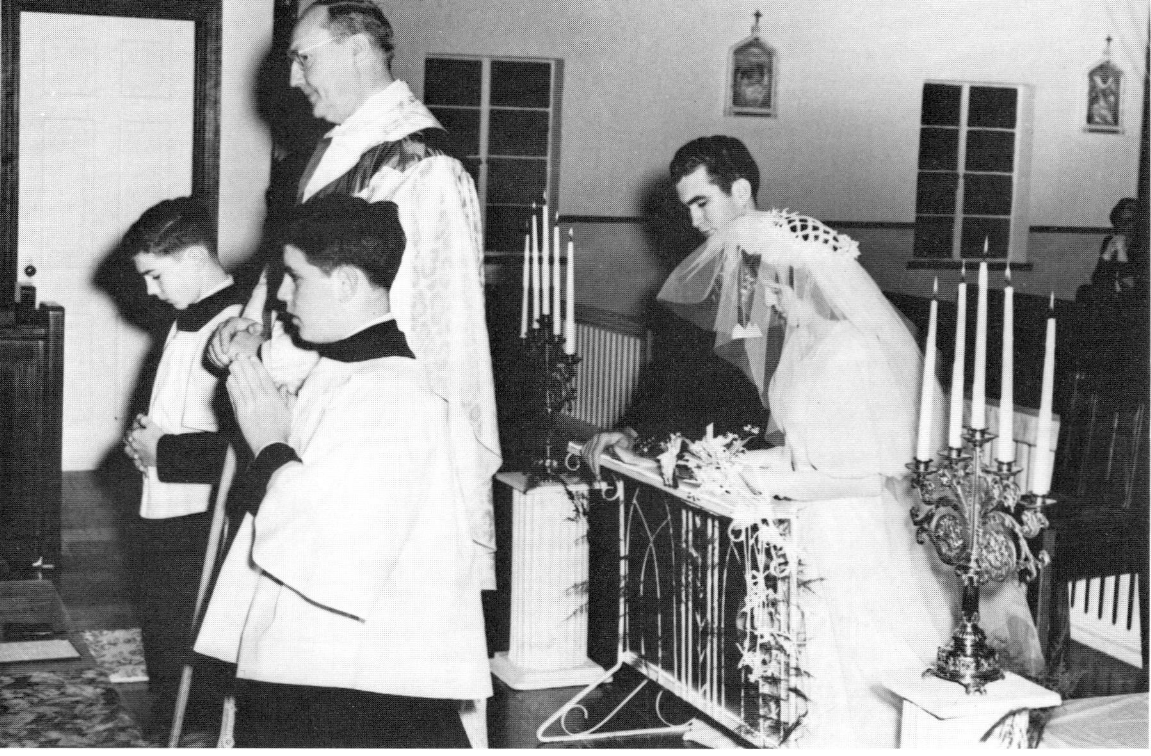

maintained a friendship with Dr. J. Frank Norris, Fort Worth's most controversial and talked-about clergyman.

1938 was the fiftieth anniversary of the laying of the St. Patrick cornerstone. The church was, by that time, a fixture in the landscape of the city. Growth of Catholic institutions since 1910 had not been rapid. A parish, Our Mother of Mercy, had been opened for black Catholics and entrusted to the Josephite Fathers. The church was built in 1930, and the school opened in 1931. The Sisters of the Holy Ghost had come from San Antonio to staff it. St. Thomas Church had been opened the previous year, 1937, to serve the needs of the Czech-speaking Catholics who had settled principally on the North Side. There was no school there, but the pastor, Father E. J. Gerlich, was making plans for one. In 1926 the Claretian Fathers had come to care for the Spanish-speaking Catholics of the city. The priests were Father Eugene Herran and Father Michael Noval. The church, San José, owed its beginning to a mission on Bluff Street which had been started by the Catholic Daughters of America. Court Louise had been chartered in 1913 under the leadership of its first Grand Regent, Mary A. Drake, who was Monsignor Nolan's sister. In addition to the

The church underwent some modification in 1934. Apart from the draping of the crucifixion window and the covering of the windows on either side, two steps were removed from the shelving of the altar. The statues were repainted and the side altars gilded. Monsignor Nolan stated that the intent was to bring St. Patrick's into ". . . strict accord with the liturgical demands of the Roman Catholic Church." The center aisle was covered with rubber tile flooring. *Photo courtesy of St. Patrick Cathedral Archives.*

mission and school on Bluff Street, the Catholic Daughters were also responsible for the St. Ann's Business Women's Club which operated at a fine home for working women on Penn Street. It opened in 1929. In 1928 the Vincentian Fathers and the Brothers of the Sacred Heart withdrew from St. Mary's and Laneri. The Benedictines of New Subiaco Abbey in Arkansas took their place, thus beginning an exceedingly fruitful ministry in Fort Worth which would last for fifty years.

The years of the forties were to be a time of rapid growth for the Church in a city transformed by war. But in 1938 there were few in the depression-bound city who could picture such a thing. Monsignor Nolan and his assistants, Father Langenhorst and Father Felderhoff, were tending to the crowded Mass schedule and to the care of the school. They were dispensing such charity as they could afford and counting the nickels in the collection in hopes of paying the bills. St. Patrick's was, even then, a second parish for most of the Catholics of the city. Its downtown location at the hub of public transportation made it accessible to all, and the Mass schedule suited almost anyone's needs. Monsignor Nolan was aging—indeed, he died the following year. The church was aging, too. People now called it "Old St. Patrick's," for it was older than most of the city's Catholics. It looked it. Photographs from the time give the impression of a somewhat run-down building. The people of Fort Worth, however, Catholic and non-Catholic alike, had grown to love the place and to respect its aging pastor who had been so much a part of things for such a long time.

Monsignor Nolan was buried on Wednesday, December 27, 1939. His death occurred on Christmas Eve of that year. In mid-December he had gone with Bishop Lynch on a trip to Texarkana and Tyler. While in Tyler he was hospitalized briefly for bronchitis. Upon his return to Fort Worth he had resumed his duties up until the evening of December 18. Shortly before midnight he had a cerebral hemorrhage. Recognizing the gravity of his condition, Father Langenhorst administered the last rites of the church. Nolan was taken to St. Joseph's Hospital where he remained until his death on the 24th.

The funeral Mass was celebrated by the Rt. Rev. Msgr. B. H. Diamond of Sacred Heart Cathedral in Dallas. Father Henry Felderhoff was deacon, and Father Clair McTamney was subdeacon. Monsignor Wendelin Nold of Dallas preached the sermon, and Bishop Lynch presided and pronounced the final absolution. Archbishop Gerken of Santa Fe conducted the graveside rites at Mount Olivet. Bishops Byrne of Galveston and Garriga of Corpus Christi were present. Almost all the clergy of the Diocese of Dallas and many priests from other parts of the state and beyond were in attendance.

The list of pallbearers, active and honorary, is a cross section of parishioners and of distinguished Fort Worth citizens: Dr. Leo Phillips, Bill Costello, George Gleeson, William Margowski, James O'Connel, Bernard Smith, W. B. Renfro, and George J. Kreyenbuhl; also, T. P. O'Gara, George S. Herney, James F. O'Hara, F. B. Thompson, C. D. Shepard, John E. Duffy, Ben Winslett, Stan Fenelon, Thomas P. Fenelon, M. A. O'Brien, A. J. O'Brien, P. Bert O'Connel, Thomas Leahy, Raymond Finn;

Amon Carter, John P. Shannon, James M. North, Jr., James R. Record, Dr. Jack Daly, Dr. Webb Walker, A. L. Schuman, Dr. Alden Coffey, Henry G. Bowden, Dr. Thomas Goodman, James T. Tuohy, H. C. Trentman, H. Veal Jewell, Walter Duffey, A. G. Donovan, Dave Donoghue, Dr. E. M. Waits, Fritz G. Lanham, R. E. Harding, Ben E. Keith, Marvin D. Evans, T. J. Harrell.

Among them, too, were Ellis Boyd, J. J. Hurley, W. J. Bailey, W. J. Marsh, George Eagle, William Parr, Jr., William P. Higgins, A. C. Broussard, P. J. Conway, Arthur J. Doherty, J. B. Patterson, Elmer Renfro, Walter B. Scott, W. C. Stonestreet, Bob Sweeney, Rev. J. R. Thompson, W. A. Hanger, John B. Collier, Jr., Dr. J. T. Edwards, A. J. Fulkerson;

William Monnig, Henry Love, W. K. Stripling, Fred P. Mueller, W. T. Ladd, Rabbi Phillip Graubart, W. C. Guthrie, W. E. Justin, Rev. L. D. Anderson, Dr. R. L. Grogan, Judge Bruce Young, Dr. C. A. Hickman, Floyd L. Carmichall, John B. Davis, H. C. Vandervoort, Dr. M. V. Cregan, Rev. Charles G. Fox, Paul McDermott, Rev. J. R. Maceo, Rev. J. N. R. Score, Dr. L. A. Bernhardi, Harry D. Vinnedge, Jack Wilkinson and Bruce Vawter, Sr.

PEACE! FIRI

LARGEST CIRCULATION
IN TEXAS
OVER 175,000 DAILY

FORT WORTH STAR-'

(CTS)—Chicago Tribune Service ● (CDN)—Chicago Daily News
(NANA)—North American Newspaper Alliance

A Fort Worth Owned Newspape

SIXTY-FIFTH YEAR, NO. 196.

FORT WORTH, TEXAS ••• Where the West Begins ••• WEDNE

Japanese Accept Te

Indianapolis Is Sunk With Loss of 883

Heavy Cruiser Torpedoed By Japanese Submarine In Philippines Sea

BY MORRIE LANDSBERG.

PELELIU, Palau Islands, Aug. 5 (Delayed) (AP).—The 10,000-ton cruiser Indianapolis was sunk in less than 15 minutes, presumably by a Japanese submarine, 12 minutes past midnight July 30—and 883 crew members lost their lives in one of the Navy's worst disasters.

She went down in the Philippines Sea, within 450 miles of Leyte while on an unescorted high speed run from San Francisco.

The fatal torpedo attack came without a second's warning. Two explosions flashed out of her bow. She quivered while flames streaked like a white glowing tongue down passageways all through her slim hull.

In less than 15 minutes the Indianapolis was gone; 10,000 tons of "proud and happy" ship plunged headfirst into the sea.

Nobody outside the oil-covered circle of men and debris in the water knew her fate until after a Peleliu search plane led the way to the rescue of the 315 men who survived five days in the sea.

Nearly 700 men went down with the ship. Hundreds more jumped off the cruiser's rearing side in time—but many were without life preservers or rafts, without clothing, without hope of remaining afloat for long.

A total of 883 crew members lost

OFFERS PRAYER—Pvt. George Beaudoux, 18, of Whittier, Cal., collapsed in the arms of Msgr. Joseph G. O'Donohoe of St. Patrick's Catholic Church Tuesday soon after receiving word of the Japs' surrender. On a troop train which paused here to allow the men to celebrate the peace announcement, Beaddoux kept repeating, "if only my brother had lived to see this day." His brother, Marine Corp. Robert Beaudoux, was killed on Iwo Jima. Private Beaudoux received permission of the train commander to seek a church to offer his prayers. (Staff Photo).

CITY CELEBRATES JOYOUSLY, NOISILY

Fleet Gets Orders to Quit War

Planes in Air Ready To Drop Bombs on Tokio Called Back.

GUAM, Wednesday, Aug. 15 (AP). Orders have been issued to the U. S. Pacific Fleet and to other forces under command of the commander in chief of the U. S. Pacific Fleet to cease offensive operations against the Japanese, Admiral Nimitz announced Wednesday.

The announcement was made in a very brief communique issued at 11 a. m.—exactly three hous after President Truman's announcement that Japan had accepted surrender terms.

Nimitz did not disclose at what time his order was issued to all fleet units and other forces under his command.

However, the order had been radioed to Admiral Halsey's 3rd Fleet, off Honshu, almost immediately—barely in time to prevent carrier pilots from unloading hundreds of tons of bombs on the Tokio area.

Reports direct from the fleet said "hundreds of carrier planes were but a few seconds from their targets" when their planes' radioes told them of the truce.

"It looks like the war is over. Cease firing, but if you see any enemy planes in the air shoot them down in friendly fashion," Halsey himself radioed the fliers.

The pilots jettisoned their bombs into the waters off Honshu.

Another dispatch, from Okinawa, said one of the war's biggest mis-

GENI

MacARTI
NIPPON

MANILA, Wednesday, (INS). — General MacArt

WAR AND PEACE

The century of the existence of St. Patrick's saw two major wars and a number of lesser ones. The life of the parish and of the whole community was deeply affected. The First World War was a cause of some bewilderment. Irish Americans, in particular, thought that it was "England's war" and saw no need to become involved. However, once the United States entered the war, the spirit of patriotism was universal, and many prayers were offered at St. Patrick's for victory and peace. Three Army Air Force training fields operated in Tarrant County, and Arlington Heights was the site of Camp Bowie, a large U. S. Army training base. Thousands of American and French soldiers were trained there.

The Second World War, because of its duration and global extent, involved the American people totally, and St. Patrick's did its part. The parishioners of those days saw new early Masses added to the schedule to accommodate workers on the round-the-clock shifts at the Consolidated Vultee bomber plant. They welcomed the relaxation of the laws of fasting and abstinence brought about by food rationing. Evening Masses made their appearance at that time. Pope Pius XII authorized them for the sake of ministry to the millions of service-men and women. The clergy of St. Patrick's did their part in this pastoral effort. A large service flag was blessed and raised above the statue of the Sacred Heart in the sanctuary. It bore a star for each man and woman from the parish in the military service of the nation. Eventually, there were more than 700 stars on the flag.

All followed the progress of the war very closely. As the time drew near for the invasion of Europe in 1944, Monsignor O'Donohoe scheduled two special services for

First Fridays, a morning Mass of reparation and a noon Mass for the remission of sins. He pointed out, "This Mass usually is celebrated before some great event when God's favor publicly is sought . . . . With the invasion of the continent imminent, it is felt that this Mass would be most opportune." The Mass intentions column of the bulletins of the time lists Mass after Mass requested by anxious families for the safety of loved ones at the front and

Every church had its service flag. Blue stars represented men and women in the armed forces. Gold stars stood for those who gave their lives.
Photo courtesy of The University of Texas at Arlington Libraries.

Opposite Page:

Photo courtesy of The University of Texas at Arlington Libraries.

The Blessed Virgin's altar was a focal point
for prayers for peace and safety.
*Photo courtesy of The University of Texas at
Arlington Libraries.*

for their speedy return. At the end of
the war, a life sized crucifix was
placed near the main doors of the
church for those who had lost their
lives.

****

Throughout the war, an
arrangement of blue votive lights was
kept burning perpetually before the
Marian altar. It was the site of many
special prayers and also of the
spiritual exercises of a group of
young women called the "Victory
Girls." They were members of a
group sponsored by the Catholic
Community Service of the United
Service Organization (USO),
dedicated to the entertainment of
the host of servicemen, far from
home, stationed near Fort Worth and
at Camp Wolters in Mineral Wells.
More than 300 girls joined, many of
them from O.L.V. and St. Joseph's
School of Nursing. Monsignor
O'Donohoe was chaplain of the
group, and Mrs. Alicia Fenelon White
and Miss Margaret Collins were the
sponsors. The Knights of Columbus
held an open house for service
people each Sunday afternoon. A
news article of the time tells of a
group of servicemen invited to
breakfast at St. Patrick's rectory.

****

St. Patrick's Church was preparing
for Solemn Vespers for the Vigil of
the Assumption, August 14, 1945,
when word was flashed by radio that
Japan had accepted the terms of
surrender. The front doors of the
church were flung wide open, and
people began to stream into the
twilight interior—men and women
with tears in their eyes, tense-faced
soldiers wearing their battle stars,
elderly women with mantillas over
their heads, family groups—all
heeding an inner impulse to enter
the church and return thanks. Shifts
of bell ringers tugged at the bell
ropes, sending the peal of bells out
over the city to mingle with the
honking horns, the guns, and the
giant firecrackers.

As the procession of clergy reached the altar to begin the service, the organ burst forth into "The Star-Spangled Banner" whose words soared to the vaulted ceiling and wafted out onto the crowded downtown streets. More and more people arrived, Catholics and Protestants, many of them parents, wives, sweethearts, and children of men in uniform, living and dead. Bishop Byrne of Galveston, the guest celebrant, gave the Benediction, and the service closed with the whole church singing "America." Monsignor O'Donohoe then thanked God that there were only four gold stars among the hundreds of stars on the church's service flag.

The church was draped in red, white, and blue in celebration of victory in 1945. J. J. Langever of Fort Worth arranged the flags of the victorious allied nations in the center aisle.
Photo courtesy of The University of Texas at Arlington Libraries.

CHAPTER 4

Nature Abhors a Straight Line

In January and February of 1946, the aging St. Patrick's Church took on a new lease on life and beauty. For the first time since the church was built in 1888, the whole interior of the structure was renovated and redecorated. The church had originally been lit by gas, although electricity was installed soon after it was built. By 1945, however, new wiring in conduits was needed throughout the building. It was done. A maze of steel scaffolding, the most elaborate ever seen in Fort Worth aside from the Convair plant, was assembled to reach the sixty-one foot high ceiling. The crew of forty workmen, having removed all the old plaster, found that seventy-five percent of the original metal lathe, itself the first ever used in North Texas, was reusable with the addition of pencil rod to make it fall-proof. The plasterers required approximately three railcar loads of acoustical plaster and zonalite to complete the job. They applied an oyster white plaster to the ceilings. The walls were done in a neutral tone. The job, which they promised would be completed in six weeks, was done by H. I. Moreland, general contractor, with Condron and Richards having the plastering contract. It was a big project by anyone's standards. A whole week was required just to erect the scaffolding. Painting was a big part of the project. The dome of the apse, which had been blue and green with gold angels, was repainted in sky blue and ivory with flesh-colored angels. The ceiling beams and window frames were walnut-grained, and new confessionals were built and installed.

The priest who initiated this renovation saw it simply as the first step in a series of projects which would greatly alter the church. His St. Patrick's would present a new face to the city and world. Not only would it look different, but its whole style would be different. He had a mind full of ideas of what the church could be and a heart full of impressions of devotion and beauty seen or heard of in distant places and times gone by. In a letter of 1952, he wrote: "Nature abhors a straight line—God is the author of nature—therefore, God prefers baroque with its curvaceous lines flowing and graceful curves." He wanted to make his ideas incarnate in stone, glass, wood, metal, and lace at St. Patrick's. He wanted to make the richness of Catholicism with all its varied traditions visible for all to see. And that is what he proceeded to do.

He was Joseph Grundy O'Donohoe, and he had known St. Patrick's Church all his life. He was born in Fort Worth on November 18, 1893. His father was Michael Charles O'Donohoe, born in Ireland, and his mother was Mary Virginia Humphreys O'Donohoe from Ozark, Arkansas. Born in a brick house at the corner of East Weatherford and Jones Streets, O'Donohoe attended the First Ward Elementary School and then high school in the same building, since the high school building on Jennings Avenue had burned. He was eighteen when he graduated in 1911. That was an important spring in his life, because in March of that year he was received into the Catholic Church at St. Patrick's. Father Vitus Graffeo, the assistant priest, baptized him. His godfather was the pastor, Father Robert M. Nolan. Old-time parishioners remember that he used to be around the church a lot as a boy.

The newly-Catholic Grundy O'Donohoe went to the University of Dallas on Oak Lawn Avenue in that city. The school yearbook remarks that his best subject was Latin, that he spent most of his free time working in the Mexican missions of Dallas, and that his fellow students nicknamed him "deacon." It also reports that he

was a connoisseur of pastries and desserts. He received his degree in 1915, entered Kenrick Seminary in St. Louis, and quickly completed his studies there. Bishop Lynch ordained him priest at Sacred Heart Cathedral, Dallas, on June 7, 1917. His early assignments were Waxahachie, where he was pastor for ten years and then Sherman, where he served for twelve years. He was a frequent visitor to Fort Worth and St. Patrick's.

Father O'Donohoe was deeply interested in Church history and worked at it. In 1925 he became secretary of the Knights of Columbus Historical Commission which compiled a multi-volume history of the Church in Texas from 1519 to the twentieth century. In 1935 the six bishops of the state chose him to plan and implement the Catholic exhibit at the 1936 Texas Centennial Exposition on the Fair Grounds in Dallas. He was also an inveterate traveler, making several visits to Spain, Italy, and Jerusalem and often going to Mexico where part of his family resided. In his studies and his travels he learned, saw, and bought objects of beauty that came to his attention. Beautiful images, vessels, and vestments began to turn up at St. Patrick's as dreams came true in his own

home church. He researched all these objects carefully. He knew what he was doing and why. After his death Father Thomas McGrath, a Jesuit priest who knew him well, said this about him: "Although a convert to the Church, there was not the slightest trace of Protestant background in his make-up. You would think that he drank the Catholic faith with his mother's milk. His love for the Blessed Mother made him love the Rosary and caused him to keep a vigil light burning before her statue continuously. And the monsignor was never happier or more at home than when surrounded by his fellow priests. Any priest was always most welcome in his home."

O'Donohoe once wrote an open letter to the *Southern Messenger*, a Catholic newspaper read throughout the state, which reveals much about his thoughts, his values, and his policies at St. Patrick's consequent upon those values. The letter was a plea for the use of blue liturgical vestments on feasts of the Blessed Virgin Mary. White represented her purity, but white represented a lot of other things as well; and he wanted her to have a color of her own. He wrote:

> The greater part of the Catholic world, geographically speaking, at least, uses blue for the liturgical color on Mary's feasts. Some may retort that this is a Spanish custom, but it's high time Catholics in this country lost that Protestant engendered antipathy toward everything Spanish. It's worse than a relic of provincialism to disparage things Spanish in this day of such world wide dissemination of knowledge and enlightenment, yet how much crass ignorance is displayed amongst our very own when Mexico, South America, the Philippines, or the Antilles are mentioned in discussion, or, worse still, when a defense of the Church in the country first mentioned is attempted.
>
> From the twelfth century down to the Protestant Reformation which so completely blighted that delicate and beautiful flower of English piety and devotion to the Holy Mother of God, blue was a popular liturgical color in Mary's dowry. In our own country in the states of Texas, New Mexico, Arizona, California, and Florida this beautiful color dignified the celebration of Our Lady's festivals until after the American occupation when French bishops and priests superseded the old Spanish and Mexican missionaries.

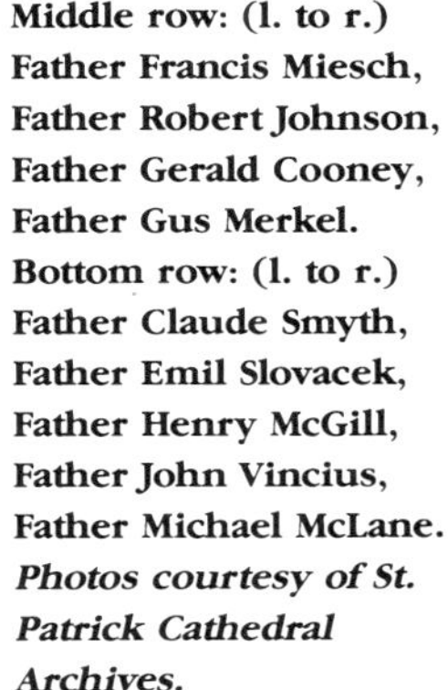

Father Thomas Tschoepe. His first appointment was as assistant at St. Patrick's Church in 1943. *Photo courtesy of* The Texas Catholic.

Father Joseph Vann and Father Carl Vogel were assistants to Monsignor O'Donohoe. Father Vann is buried in the crypt chapel at St. Patrick's. *Photo courtesy of St. Patrick Cathedral Archives.*

Middle row: (l. to r.) Father Francis Miesch, Father Robert Johnson, Father Gerald Cooney, Father Gus Merkel. Bottom row: (l. to r.) Father Claude Smyth, Father Emil Slovacek, Father Henry McGill, Father John Vincius, Father Michael McLane. *Photos courtesy of St. Patrick Cathedral Archives.*

Rome's permission can be elicited by our bishops' petitioning for the same, and such action can be brought about by a deep and concerted interest on the part of Mary's clients and children throughout this country.

Although the bishops did not act on his suggestion, Monsignor O'Donohoe was ready. St. Patrick's sacristy was equipped with more than one complete, solemn set of blue vestments, and one hears that they were occasionally used. As for the French bishops and priests who had changed the old Spanish ways—well, one of them had built the distinctly un-Spanish St. Patrick's, and where he had failed, O'Donohoe could make it right!

In 1947 the main altar was redone and the side altars replaced. The work was done in Lent. Father Lawrence Breedlove, then a high-school student attending 7:00 a.m. Mass each morning, recalls the project and the big pieces of marbleized, molded plaster standing about the church waiting to be assembled. The tabernacle was removed from the main altar and made into an ambry for the oils. A new tabernacle and the

The original Marian altar. Mrs. Dominic Rappich is shown presenting her bridal bouquet October 31, 1945.
Photo courtesy of Mrs. Maggie Rappich.

The new Marian Altar
which was installed in
1947 (1988 photo).
*Photo courtesy of St.
Patrick Cathedral/David
Barros photographer.*

superstructure above the high altar were added. The large statue of Our Lady of the Apocalypse which dominates the church was placed atop the reredos. The side altars were removed and replaced by the present ones of wood and plaster with a marble finish. The new side altars were designed to match the arrangement in the center of the sanctuary. The communion rail, of the same material, matched the altars. At the same time, the altars flanking the main entrance were added. They feature images of the Sorrowful Mother and of Christ crucified. At one time there was an inner vestibule in the narthex which helped to keep an even temperature in the building. It had long since been removed. There were more statues in the church than there are today, including a shrine in the south vestibule area. Many of the statues were in the Spanish or Mexican style which the pastor so admired. Saints canonized during his pastorate were honored and their images introduced into the church; for example, St. Frances Xavier Cabrini and St. Maria Goretti. The paintings of Mary of Agreda and of the Venerable Antonio Margil above the vestibule doors attest to Monsignor O'Donohoe's interest in the history of the Church in Texas. Much of the available wall space was given over to verses, biblical and otherwise, which were lettered on the surfaces at eye level.

Of the original furnishings of the church only the main altar itself, the stations, the pews, and baptismal font remained after the refurbishing was done. Of course, there was the stained glass, or most of it. Remarking that the crucifixion window was invisible from inside after sundown, and that at evening services only a dark area could be seen above the tabernacle, he had the window covered and a beautiful, devotional crucifix hung in its place. For a time, above the tabernacle there stood a large image of Our Lady of Mount Carmel, a special devotion of Monsignor O'Donohoe. Jesús Paez, a young man who worked for Monsignor for years and was closely associated with him until his death, told of his returning from a trip to Europe with a determination to electrify everything. "The angels in the church used to have candles, and he electrified them. The votive lights in the church were also electrified. You would put in a quarter and push a button to light the candle. I would have to put them out after Mass, and everyone would be angry at me because their candle was being put out. They proved impractical so we changed back to regular candles."

A newly acquired crucifix is blessed by Father Lawrence DeFalco, assistant pastor from 1942 to 1952. This crucifix is no longer in St. Patrick's Church. *Photo courtesy of St. Patrick Cathedral Archives.*

Many other interesting stories are told about O'Donohoe. Al Becan, who served his Mass in the 1940's, said the 1946 replastering of the church was occasioned by the collapse of part of the ceiling. He recalls that it happened at the early Mass on a cold Saturday morning. About two minutes into the Mass Monsignor O'Donohoe stopped the prayers of the Mass and told the people in the back of the church to move up front. Everyone did except one man. Monsignor stopped again and said, "I told you to move up." This time the man did. Becan said that about halfway through the Mass there was a loud crashing sound. The plaster from the ceiling of the choir loft and one-fourth of the body of the church had fallen to the floor. Becan said there was no previous indication that the ceiling was likely to fall, and that Monsignor O'Donohoe attributed his moving the people up front to inspiration.

Not everyone liked what he did. Some thought the church overdone. There were those who thought some of the features grotesque. But the parishioners, in general, admired him and accepted his leadership, for he was present to them and attentive. He was a truly distinctive individual and a person of intelligence, imagination, energy, and devotion. Like him or not, no one could ignore him or ever forget him.

Such was the priest who came from Sherman to be pastor of St. Patrick's in January of 1940, only a few days after Monsignor Nolan was buried.

****

There was war in Europe and Asia in 1940, and in 1941 the United States entered the conflict. The war changed the nation forever. Fort Worth changed, too, and Fort Worth's Catholic community was transformed. Many individuals and families were on the move. Jobs were available as they had not been for more than a decade. The city was an important hub of the war effort, possessing military installations as well as a large bomber plant. Many Catholic families moved into the area in the early years of the war, fine Catholic families that became valued members of the parishes of the city. It was clear that the existing parishes were insufficient to serve the growing population. Two new parishes were founded early in the war. 1941 saw the beginning of St. George Parish in the Riverside area of the city.

In 1942 Father Ernest Langenhorst, who had served as assistant priest at St. Patrick's since his ordination in 1930, was appointed to organize St. Alice Parish, which comprised a part of Arlington Heights and the growing neighborhoods further west. By the erection of these parishes and the redrawing of boundary lines, St. Patrick's was much reduced in size. The parish boundaries have remained substantially the same since that year.

Also, in 1941, San Mateo Parish was started by and for the railroad workers, largely Spanish-speaking people, who lived in the neighborhood north of the Texas and Pacific yards. Over the years San Mateo has been closely associated with St. Patrick's, as it is today, with many parishioners of both parishes feeling equally at home in either church.

****

A parish directory, published in 1949, reveals that there were many active organizations in the parish at mid-century and also gives the names of some of the active parishioners. Mr. W. J. Marsh was choir director and organist, assisted by Miss Patricia Keith. Choir members were: Bill Parr, Carlos Villalobo, Charles Bray, Nolan Havens, Bernard Lunt, Mrs. Stephen Brady, Mrs. L. G. O'Hara, Miss Mae Marsh, Miss Frances Oechsner, Miss Patricia Evans, Raymond Stuart, Joe Scudiero, Patrick Fee, and L. Marcella. Also singing were Mrs. Ethel Greer, Mrs. Frank Parker, Miss Mary Jane Higgins, and Miss Verdi Carter.

There was a Holy Name society whose officers were Walter P. Klein, Thomas Bartula, and Anthony E. Witkowski. Father James Meuree was moderator of the St. Vincent de Paul. The officers were F. J. Greiner, A. E. Witkowski, and Frank Yeager. There was a Parish Council headed by Mrs. David Bellew, Mrs. Harry J. Bernhardt, Mrs. D. T. Costello, and Mrs. George B. Zimpleman. Mrs. J. M. Kimport was in charge of retreats; Mrs. Henry C. Owen dealt with the CCD. Mrs. H. Clemmons headed the study clubs, and Mrs. A. B. Gathings supervised the distribution of Catholic literature. Mrs. Owen and Miss Patricia Peninger were librarians.

There was a St. Ignatius Mother's Club whose officers were Mrs. Rufus Parr, Mrs. Hugh Helbig, Mrs. Julian Jones, Mrs. Mary Evelyn Tomlin, and Mrs. A. J. Griffith. Officers of the Sodality of the B.V.M. were Misses Rosa Paez, Elizabeth Ann Parr, Margie Lambright, and Jean Carter. Third

Order of St. Francis officers were Joseph S. Noel, Mrs. Mary Joseph Fanning, and Mrs. Owen.

The St. Patrick's Club was part of the life of the parish for many years. Its leaders were Mrs. Leonard Davidson, Mrs. W. J. Koppa, Mrs. Maurice Egan, Mrs. F. H. Scouten, Mrs. Lee Etta Schuhard, and Mrs. A. J. Gilstrap.

The staff of the Confraternity of Christian Doctrine included Father Meuree, Father DeFalco, J. C. Rich, Mrs. F. J. Greiner, Mrs. Mary Horan, Mrs. Henry C. Owen, Miss Josephine Greiner, Miss Beatrice Meter, Miss Verdi Carter, Miss Irene Witkowski, and Miss Patricia Peninger. Ed. J. Steiner was president of the Calvary Cemetery Association, and Margaret Lehane was prefect of both the Purgatorial Society and the League of the Sacred Heart.

Not only was a new appearance given to the church itself, but changes were also made beneath the floor. Excavations beneath the church were undertaken to provide room for many things. Quite a large basement area was opened up. Public restrooms were installed there. A parish library and a room for small meetings were provided downstairs. One of the main purposes of the digging was to have a small chapel and mausoleum. It was done, and the chapel, named All Souls, was used for frequent exposition and adoration of the Blessed Sacrament and occasionally for weekday Masses. The altar in the chapel is believed to be one of the original side altars from the church. The whole underground area could be reached by steps on both the north and south sides of the church. The access on the south side opposite the rectory was marked by a sign "Watch Thy Step." It was a necessary caution, for the ceilings were low, and anyone approaching six feet in height had to be extremely careful. Monsignor O'Donohoe was himself quite short and could move about the area freely.

In the excavation project the mausoleum was uppermost in O'Donohoe's mind. He intended to be buried there himself, and he wanted to rebury Father Guyot there first. The final resting place for Father Guyot was to be in the concrete and stone support of the high altar directly overhead. O'Donohoe's own resting place was to be in the north wall of the chapel. The reinterment of Father Guyot was a matter of some delicacy. Monsignor O'Donohoe's practice was to celebrate significant occasions in grand style. But this significant act was carried out privately without publicity or pomp. The only persons present when the reburial took place were O'Donohoe himself, Father DeFalco, William P. Higgins, a highly respected Catholic layman, Margaret Lehane, the sacristan, John Houts, the custodian, and Guy Thompson, who carried out the project. Further information about the crypt chapel is found in another section of the book.

Another significant occasion was carried out with all the splendor Monsignor O'Donohoe could muster. This was the reception in Fort Worth of Bishop Thomas K. Gorman on Sunday, May 11, 1952. Bishop Gorman had just been appointed Co-adjutor Bishop of the Diocese of Dallas and had taken over the administration of the diocese from Bishop Lynch who was incapacitated by age and infirmity. Monsignor O'Donohoe was impressed by Bishop Gorman. He wrote to a friend: "Bishop Gorman is a wonderfully fine man who means business. He is so kind and considerate and appreciative of everything done for him. He was just wonderful over here in Fort Worth the Sunday he spent with us." He determined to receive the new Bishop with great honor and to make his visit to Fort Worth memorable. He was one of the few who could recall the day forty-two years before when the newly consecrated Bishop Lynch had come to the city and to St. Patrick's.

The plans for the welcoming called for a "military" Mass at St. Patrick's at 10:00 a.m. and a civic reception honoring the new bishop at Will Rogers Auditorium at 3:00 p.m. The officers of the Mass were Father L. M. DeFalco, celebrant, Benedictine Fathers Leonard Knoff and Fintan Oldham, deacon and subdeacon, and Father Carl Vogel, master of ceremonies. The choir sang W. J. Marsh's "Assumption Mass." Before Mass there was a ceremony of the tendering of obedience to the new bishop. Representatives of groups and organizations would have the opportunity to welcome Bishop Gorman and to offer their loyalty.

First came a group of small children from St. Ignatius, dressed as angels, to present an impressive spiritual bouquet of collected prayers and sacrifices. They were followed by a group of preschool children dressed in caps and gowns. Then came the dean, Monsignor himself, followed by the priests, the acolytes, the sisters of the various religious congregations, then representatives of parish societies and sodalities.

A group of men brought an ancient, life-size crucifix to the Bishop. They were accompanied by Mrs. Nenetta B. Carter, Mrs. Catherine Lehane, 93, who had been present when St. Patrick's Church was dedicated, and a group of ladies dressed in deep black with black lace mantillas, who presented a purse to the Bishop and offered the obedience of the parish.

After this presentation, there came the officers of the societies, confraternities, and city-wide groups: the Holy Name Society, the St. Vincent de Paul Society, the Ushers' Society, the Third Order of St. Francis, the League of the Sacred Heart, the Children of Mary, the Confraternity of Prayer and Penance, the Peoples' Eucharistic League, and the Purgatorial Society. Then came the Calvary Cemetery Association, the Marthas, the Ladies of St. Patrick's Club, and the National Council of Catholic Women. Each group carried its banner. The officers entered the sanctuary and knelt before the Bishop while the members stood at the communion rail in testimony. All women approaching the Bishop that day were required to dress in "deep black with a black lace mantilla," for, as Monsignor O'Donohoe wrote: "It is a distinguished honor for a woman to be permitted in the sanctuary while divine services are being celebrated and the most decorous manner of dress should be observed on such an occasion."

Next came the nonparochial groups: representatives of Scout Troop No. 32, then the two councils of the Knights of Columbus, Monsignor Nolan 759 and Bishop Dunne 1189, then the Catholic Daughters, both the state officers and those of Court Louise, and the officers of the Laneri Boosters Club. In short, the whole multifaceted Catholic community of Fort Worth was presented to the new Bishop.

The best remembered part of the Mass came at the elevation of the Sacred Host and Precious Blood, when the military guard of honor fired a salute inside, and a salvo of bombs was detonated on the towers outside. Guy Thompson, in a recent interview said: "The effect was terrifying. Father DeFalco, the celebrant, was so startled that he broke the host in two. There was dead silence for a moment, and then every child in the church started crying. Across the street the telephone operators said to one another, 'How those Catholics do celebrate Mother's Day!' " For it

was on Mother's Day that Bishop Gorman first came to Fort Worth. An unscheduled 11:00 a.m. Mass that day was offered on the rectory porch due to the length of the Mass of welcome.

The Bishop and clergy had lunch at 1:00 p.m. in the rectory. The civic reception at 3:00 p.m. featured an invocation by Monsignor O'Donohoe, a welcome by Mayor Edwards, and an address by Bishop Gorman. This civic reception was arranged by an interparochial committee composed of Jack Lewis of St. George, Joseph A. Durkin of St. Alice, Frank Crumley of St. Mary's, William Jacobs of Holy Name, and Don Wallace of St. Patrick's; and by committees of the two K. C. Councils whose members were Frank Mills, Charles Gallegher, Bill Higgins, Emil LeGesse, Herbert Manning, and Dominic Rappich.

At 5:00 p.m. the Deanery Council of Catholic Women sponsored a reception for the new Bishop at the Crystal Ballroom of the Texas Hotel. Mrs. Charles Faust, diocesan president, and Mrs. James Parker, deanery president, were in the reception line. Choral groups from Our Lady of Victory Academy and Mount Carmel Academy sang, accompanied by Miss Magdalen Franko and Miss Maria Carmen Trujillo.

At 8:00 p.m. the Serra Club of Fort Worth tendered a banquet, also at the Texas Hotel. Mrs. Joseph Bandor was in charge of ticket sales. Four hundred had been sold at $3.50 at

New aluminum wheels were made for the two 2,000 pound bells atop St. Patrick's Church. They replaced wooden wheels which could not withstand the weather. The bells bear the names "Maria Assumpta" and "Maria Gloriosa." The man in coat and hat is S. M. Baker who cast the wheels. They were designed by J. J. Houts (leaning against the bell), who was in charge of maintenance in Monsignor O'Donohoe's day.
Photo courtesy of The University of Texas at Arlington Libraries.

the doors of the churches, and the ballroom was filled. Father DeFalco acted as toastmaster. Victor Simon gave the address of welcome, and E. F. Freeman introduced Bishop Gorman.

At the conclusion of the long day Bishop Gorman described it as "a reception the like of which I have never in my life witnessed anywhere." This writer attended the welcoming ceremonies in Dallas the Thursday preceding, and they couldn't hold a candle to Fort Worth's. Monsignor O'Donohoe had planned it from beginning to end and had thought out every detail. He did the Catholics of Fort Worth proud that day!

****

Weekly parish bulletins were being published at St. Patrick's in the 1940's and 1950's and offer a view of what was going on in the parish. In September of 1945 the Sunday Masses were scheduled at 5:30, 6:30, 8:00, 10:00 and 12:00 Noon. The 10:00 a.m. Mass was a Solemn Mass. Weekday Masses were at 6:30, 7:00, 7:30, and 8:00 each day. The bulletin of September 9, 1945, announced that the Solemn Mass that day was a Mass of Thanksgiving for victory and peace. There was to be a Solemn Requiem Mass on Monday at 10:00 a.m. for the heroic war dead as a tribute from priests and people to their memory. A life-size, wood carved crucifix was to be blessed at that Mass and carried in procession to the main entrance of the church where it would be placed. People were invited to pray there. That bulletin observed that the end of gas rationing should make more frequent attendance at Mass possible. An inquiry class was slated to begin the following month. At the request of parishioners, public thanks were expressed to St. Anthony, St. Frances Cabrini, and the Sacred Heart of Jesus for answers to prayers. Altar boys appointed for the week were: Alfred Becan, Bobby Jay, Jose Vasquez, Ricardo Vela, Daniel Becan, Carl Graves, Eugene Witkowski, Harry and Arthur Tolson, Joe and Danny Hall, Jimmy Murphy, Bobby Price, John Adger, Gene and Wade Freeman, and Rudy Dolkos. Banns of marriage were announced for James Basil Davidson and Pauline Sergi.

The bulletin for January 27, 1946, announced that the Sunday evening services had been cancelled due to the renovation of the church and that an extra Sunday morning Mass had been added at 11:00 for the same reason. "If you are wise, you will try to attend one of the early Masses." If people possessed diamonds they were not using or intending to use, they were invited to donate them. A cross of diamonds was being made for one of the finer chalices. Six more were needed. Four parishioners returned public thanks to St. Anthony of Padua for favors received.

The bulletin of June 15, 1947, requested better use of the parish library which was open on weekdays from 11:00 a.m. to 2:00 p.m. and all morning on Sunday. It cost $1.00 to belong. Corporate Communion for the Young Ladies' Sodality was at the 8:00 a.m. Mass followed by recitation of the Little Office of the Immaculate Conception and breakfast. The Third Order of St. Francis met at 7:00 p.m. in the church. The bulletin explained that "the new altars in St. Patrick's Church are of the Baroque style—the most popular style in Catholic countries and places the world over because it displays the richness of the Catholic faith, lifts up our hearts to God and encourages us to pray . . . ." That bulletin went on to discuss the crucifixion window in the sanctuary. "It cost $2500 to take down, repair and reinstate this big window, many times more than its original cost. Many

persons begged that the velvet hangings and devotional crucifix which temporarily replaced the window be left there permanently as they preferred them to the window. Some others prefer the window. As the beautiful old window had been one of the most loved sights of Fort Worth for many years, it was put back in place even though it cost more to do so than it was worth."

The bulletin of November 26, 1950, called attention to the fine and ancient icon of Christ brought back from Rome by the pastor and installed during that past week above St. Joseph's altar. "It is nearly 300 years old. The icon is surrounded by 196 tiny electric light bulbs which were also brought from Rome where they are used everywhere in the churches and shrines. The 'arty art' crowd turn up their noses at such but we ordinary humans seem to be pleased with such simple and artless decoration."

The May 13, 1951, bulletin called attention to a new statue of the Blessed Virgin which had been placed in the church. The statue was two years in the making in Mexico City. It is carved out of cedar wood, covered with gold leaf, then

In Lent of 1943 Passionist Fathers Paschal Barry and Cletus Brady preached a dialogue mission at St. Patrick's. Monsignor O'Donohoe is shown with the mission crucifix.
Photo courtesy of The University of Texas at Arlington Libraries.

painted and finally the decorative designs of the garments delicately chiseled through the paint to show the gold beneath. By 1951 Mass intentions were being announced. Some of the intentions for that week: "Stan Fenelon req. by Miss Mary Moore, Sacred Heart of Jesus req. by Mrs. Isabel Weaver, Michael Bahan req. by Mrs. Mary Bahan, Carl Ragon req. by Mrs. John Pfieffer, Mildred Rudd, intention of Mrs. Gathings, Albertine Fleming req. by Mr. and Mrs. J. R. Neil, Thanksgiving to the Sacred Heart by Frank Yeager." Other Masses were offered at the request of Miss Ernestine Scott, John A. Anderson, Miss Anne Fenelon, Mrs. Bridget Reid, Mrs. C. J. Malone, Sr., Mr. and Mrs. Bruno Lore, Miss Dorothy Witkowski, the William C. Yeager family, and Mrs. Isabel Farnsworth.

****

Monsignor O'Donohoe died shortly before midnight on January 17, 1956, after a long and debilitating illness. He died in what is now the pastor's office in St. Patrick's rectory. His bed had been brought there from his quarters on the lower level of the house because the stairs had become impossible for him. His physician, Dr. Thomas Coleman, said that he resisted hospitalization and also medication, even an aspirin, because people medicated at the end of life could not say their prayers. He died of a kidney ailment complicated by diabetes and high blood pressure, both of which he had had for many years. He was well-prepared. His will was drawn, and he had prepared instructions for his funeral and interment with his usual meticulous attention to detail.

Interviewed for this book, Jesse Paez said: "I had a daybed in here and stayed at night with him. He was always saying the rosary. He loved the chapel in the basement. I guess he knew he was going to be buried there, so he was always praying down there. The night of his death we had gone to bed, and someone woke me and told me not to be afraid, but that Monsignor had died in his sleep."

It was Father DeFalco who found him dead. Dr. Coleman and Guy Thompson came at once. They sat at the dining room table in the small hours of the morning and read his instructions for the burial.

Monsignor J. G. O'Donohoe in death. He held the rank of Protonotary Apostolic which entitled him to wear the miter, gloves, and ring. These insignia are usually associated with a bishop. *Photo courtesy of Guy Thompson.*

CRYPT

The excavated basement area of St. Patrick's Cathedral is somewhat more than half the size of the church itself. Most of the area beneath the church from the west end (Jennings Street) to approximately the halfway mark is open. The excavated area is slightly longer on the north side of the building. The area can be entered conveniently from the sacristy hallway or from the steps on the north side of the church. For many years the basement has been used for storage and as headquarters for maintenance operations. That, however, was not the original intention.

In the 1950's, the lower level was a center of parish activity. There was a meeting room there which, in the 1960's, was called the Shamrock Room. There was more headroom on the north side of the building, and the room was one that could be used comfortably. A parish library also flourished there for a while, and there were public restrooms. The excavation is shallower on the south side, and water pipes and conduits along the ceiling make walking hazardous for a tall person.

Central to the whole below-ground complex is the crypt chapel dedicated to All Souls. The chapel was designed by Monsignor O'Donohoe, who wanted priests to be buried there and who fully intended to be buried there himself. The custom of burying in a crypt or even simply below the floor of the church is an ancient one, and it was commonly done even into this century. He also intended the chapel for other purposes. It was, on occasion, used for Mass. The Serra Club held all night adoration of the Blessed Sacrament there beginning in the evening and ending at 6:30 a.m. when the Sacred Host was returned to the church above. There was a Gothic altar and illuminated plaques

Parish meetings were regularly held in the basement of the church.
Photo courtesy of St. Patrick Cathedral Archives.

of mother-of-pearl depicting scenes from the life of Christ and the mysteries of the rosary. There was a large reclining statue of Christ in the sepulchre and other devotional objects, including a kneeling statue of St. Francis of Assisi wrought with gold leaf. It was a match to the statue of St. Anthony of Padua which stands to the right of the central entrance of the main church.

The first burial was that of Father Guyot, and it presented a problem. A permit from the city was necessary lest the law be broken. Word had gotten out about the projected reburial, and an objection was raised on the grounds that it was tantamount to establishing a new cemetery; and that could not be done. It seemed there was an impasse. Then, Guy Thompson, who had been asked by Monsignor O'Donohoe to carry out the project, had an inspiration: "I don't know how it came to me, but there is a relic under the altar, and the relic is a part of a saint, a part of the body of a saint; and I therefore said, 'We

have had a cemetery in St. Patrick's since 1888. We are simply enlarging it.' And you can do that. You can buy a little cemetery and enlarge it. The City Attorney studied it and said he agreed." The necessary permit was granted.

Guy Thompson told the story of the reburial of Father Guyot. It was done on November 4, 1948, forty-one years after the burial. "We thought he would be in a wooden coffin, and there would be just a few bones, but he was buried in an oak casket in a steel vault. His body was intact. His vestments were intact." Thompson described Father Guyot as a somewhat short man with reddish hair and a beard. He was in a black cassock with purple vestments. He wore a pair of high, laced up shoes. Guy Thompson said further: "Another interesting thing we discovered when we got down to his

1845 † 1907
REVEREND
JEAN MARIE GUYOT
OSSA HUMILIATA

grave was that it was surrounded by stubs of candles about three inches long. I theorize that they stood around that grave with lighted candles. They said the prayers, then extinguished the candles and threw them in the grave—that was part of the ceremony." Father Guyot's body disintegrated when it was moved from the casket to the box Monsignor O'Donohoe had prepared for it. O'Donohoe's mother was reburied beneath the chapel floor the following year.

Another burial in the crypt mausoleum was that of Father Joseph Wesley Vann. Father Vann had served three years as assistant pastor at St. Patrick's following his ordination in 1947. He was killed in an automobile accident near Plano. He was 31 at the time of his death.

Monsignor also had a box prepared for his own burial. It was of wood, painted black with gold lettering in Latin. It was clearly unsuitable, so he was buried in a lead-coated steel casket, beautifully furnished. He had left detailed instructions about the preparation of his bier. It was most elegant, draped in black velvet with gold tassels. There was a glaze of ice on the streets when he was laid in state, and only a handful of people were present. The clergy sang Matins and Lauds from the Office for the Dead. The sun came out the day of the funeral, and the ice melted. He was buried in the crypt.

There was some opposition to the burials in the chapel on the part of a Fort Worth cemetery owner. Monsignor O'Donohoe, therefore, prepared a memo for his successors. It reads in part: "This burial permit of Father Jos. Vann should be kept as proof of the city of Fort Worth's permission for burials of priests in the burial vaults in the mortuary chapel under the sanctuary of St. Patrick's Church. Such permission was granted by the city authorities when the basement was excavated in 1945 and the vaults placed in the chapel at the time of the entombment of the mortal remains of Rev. J. M. Guyot, builder of the church."

Opposite Page:

Father Guyot's final resting place in the crypt chapel beneath the sanctuary floor. The reburial took place in November, 1948. Guy Thompson made the transfer. Mrs. Maria Virginia O'Donohoe is buried beneath the stone bearing the words "OSSA HUMILIATA."
Photo courtesy of St. Patrick Cathedral/ David Barros photographer.

Monsignor Vincent J. Wolf looks on as members of the Stanton family crown the statue of the Blessed Virgin. They are (l. to r.) Betty Ann, Rosemary, Terri, Bern and Baldy Stanton. *Photo courtesy of Baldwin Stanton.*

Monsignor Wolf presents trophies to winners of two city-wide CYO tournaments. The winners were (l. to r.) Al Morrey of St. Rita's Parish, Dennis Calcaterra and David Hinz, both of the co-cathedral parish. *Photo courtesy of Mrs. Delcie Hinz.*

onsignor Vincent J. Wolf was appointed to take the place of the deceased Monsignor O'Donohoe in the spring of 1956. He assumed his duties on Sunday, April 6, preaching at all eight Masses that day. The new pastor was an East Texan, having been born in Texarkana. He was 44 years old when he became pastor of Fort Worth's parent parish. After being ordained in Sacred Heart Cathedral in Dallas by Bishop Lynch, he spent 15 years as pastor in Tyler. During his pastorate there he directed an extensive building program and helped the parish to grow from 150 to 500 families. He came to Fort Worth from St. Pius X in Dallas. He was also diocesan director of Catholic youth and had begun the practice of holding diocese-wide youth conventions. Such annual meetings in Fort Worth, Mineral Wells, and Dallas had attracted hundreds from all parts of the diocese.

Speaking of dioceses, Fort Worth was now a part of that, for in 1954 Bishop Gorman had added the name of Fort Worth to that of Dallas in the diocesan title. As part of that change St. Patrick's became a co-cathedral. Bishop Gorman wanted to keep regular office hours in Fort Worth and to offer the services of the diocesan chancery to the city. Monsignor O'Donohoe had rented space for the purpose in a downtown office building. In addition to the office of the bishop, there was a Catholic Charities office under the direction of Father Charles Mulholland. *The Texas Catholic* had its own Fort Worth representative, Mrs. Wilma Gibbons. The Fort Worth Chancery lasted only a few years. Bishop Gorman continued to keep office hours at St. Patrick's rectory until 1962. Catholic Charities of Fort Worth, however, endured and was a strong organization when the new diocese was formed at the end of that decade.

St. Patrick's parish in 1956 was at the crossroads. Many of its former families were now members of the newer parishes around the city. School enrollment was low, and the church and rectory both had problems. The church, though beautiful, was a nineteenth century building in need of repairs and adaptations. The rectory was the same, and both required much work and expenditure. Wolf described the situation this way: "If the exterior of the church is not attended to at once, by waterproofing and coating the walls which hold so many sacred

CHAPTER 5

The Walls Hold Sacred Secrets

secrets, it will be defeated by the elements of time and become a heap of holy debris." The rectory he described as "dreary and dingy, with painted plaster hanging in streams from the ceiling."

Across the United States in mid-century, there were downtown and inner city churches faced with the same problems, for the primacy once enjoyed by the downtown areas was over. Theaters and stores were leaving. Suburbs with their shopping centers were becoming the centers of people's lives and activities. Some downtown churches became subsidized shells of their former selves. Others were abandoned and destroyed. Monsignor Wolf was determined that that not happen to St. Patrick's. He formed a committee and launched a campaign involving parishioners and the non-Catholic community alike. The campaign was called the "St. Patrick's

Restoration and Prestige Fund." A lot of money was needed, for, in addition to the improvements, it became necessary to buy St. Ignatius School and the property on which it stood. This property belonged to the Sisters of St. Mary of Namur. They needed to sell it, and the parish had necessarily to be the buyer. A price of $207,000 was agreed upon, and this was added to the amount that had to be raised.

The campaign worked. By the spring of 1960, the parish received a summary report of what had been accomplished.

The report said that the restoration and resurfacing of the exterior was complete and that year-round air-conditioning had been installed. The stained glass windows were releaded, and the crucifixion window was unveiled and illuminated. The interior of the church was repainted, and there were new

The steering committee of the "St. Patrick's Restoration and Prestige Fund." Seated, left to right, are J. M. Spreckelmeyer, Monsignor Wolf, Frank Mills, chairman, and A. H. Elshoff. Standing, left to right, Tommy Farrell, A. Martelli, Charles Drake, Joseph P. Bandor, Stephen F. Shelvey, Jr., Charles Horan, John Tipton and Louis Neilon. *Photo courtesy of St. Patrick Cathedral Archives.*

chandeliers, indirect lighting, and a public address system. The sanctuary had been enlarged by moving the communion rail outward. The sanctuary and the aisles were now covered with red velvet acrilan carpeting. There were new, sound-proof confessionals and a wrought iron baptistry grill. It said that the bishop's throne had been refinished, reupholstered, and hung with new green and gold antique satin drapes. The sanctuary furniture had also been reupholstered. The report stated that there was a new ceiling under the choir loft, that the pews had been refinished, and the kneelers recovered.

Outside the sanctuary itself the report said that the basement had been rearranged and the Shamrock Room there redecorated for use by the young people. Outside there were a new sprinkler system and stone planter boxes at the entrance of the church.

The rectory had undergone a complete renovation, had been refurnished, and had air-conditioning put in. The rectory was as it is today, except for renovations in the basement to fit it for the various uses to which it has been put over the years. George Gutjahr, a contractor who did much fine work for the church in

Frank Mills over the years has lent his talent as reader, announcer, and narrator to St. Patrick's. When it came to broadcasting he was always the key figure. *Photo courtesy of* The Texas Catholic.

those days, was of invaluable help in these projects.

****

The parish files of those years tell an interesting story about the waxen figure of the martyr, St. Expedite, which used to be in the church. The Benedictine Sisters of Clyde, Missouri, had been given the impression that the body of St. Expedite, or at least the skeleton enclosed in wax, was in St. Patrick's Co-Cathedral. They hoped to move this major relic to their convent in Kansas City where they were prepared to build a relic chapel to house it. The Bishop of Kansas City wrote to Bishop Gorman to inquire about the matter. Gorman asked Monsignor Wolf and received this reply: "Here at St. Patrick's Cathedral we have a wax figure of St. Expedite in a prostrate position. It is six feet in length. There is no record that the wax figure contains any part of the body of St. Expedite. The only relic we have is *ex ossibus* enclosed in a small reliquary." This was not what the sisters were looking for, and the matter was dropped.

****

Monsignor Wolf looked for ways to bring the message of the Church to the wider community. Invitations to speak, preside, or participate in civic and interdenominational functions were accepted. Projects of benefit to the whole community were generously sponsored. He was interested in the Texas Boys Choir, and that group used to use the third floor of the St. Ignatius Building for its meetings and practices. Sometimes the choir would participate in parish functions. Each afternoon the parish grounds were enlivened by the youthful voices heard through the open windows. "Deo Gratias" and "A Modern Texas Roundup" resounded around the block in splendid harmony.

Monsignor Wolf was no stranger to broadcasting, and he did not hesitate to use the media for the Church's message. During his stay in East Texas he had conducted a radio program and another in Dallas. Upon coming to Fort Worth, he went on television with "The Cathedral Hour" on WBAP-TV. On the program he offered the whole community an explanation of the beliefs of the Catholic Church. It was also an opportunity to give the Catholic response to the issues of the day.

The Christmas Midnight Mass was broadcast regularly on WBAP-TV with Frank Mills doing the commentary. On Christmas Eve in 1961 the large marbleized table which used to stand in the sacristy was moved to the center of the sanctuary and suitably adorned as an altar. Midnight Mass, a Solemn Mass, was celebrated facing the congregation. The people were surprised, but delighted. The viewing audience saw the Mass in a way it had never seen it before. This was a full year and more before the Second Vatican Council began its deliberations on the liturgy, several years before free-standing altars became a regular fixture in Catholic churches. St. Patrick's Cathedral was pointing the way to the future.

There was, in the early 1960's, an awakening spirit of ecumenism in the Church, and new ways were earnestly sought to reach out to those separated from the fold. St. Patrick's offered a series of dialogue sermons. The two assistants, Father Hazel and Father Hoover, would take their stand before microphones on either side of the sanctuary. One would take the Catholic position, the other that of a non-Catholic questioner. The exchanges between the two were lively and sometimes even slightly heated. For an hour the two would argue about the Eucharist, faith, or the structure Christ intended for His Church. The series was popular and well attended. Inquiry classes were large in those years, and many converts entered the Church, not only at St. Patrick's but throughout the country.

Another initiative was the ecumenical open house. The parish had a CCD board, and on a given day specially prepared persons would describe features of the church, altar, confessionals, font, and the rest, to all who came. The open houses were widely advertised, and there were many participants.

The two assistants were deeply involved in the work of the Confraternity of Christian Doctrine. Father Hoover left in January, 1962, to become diocesan director of the whole religious education effort. Father Hazel stayed a few more years and organized a Western Division Board of the CCD which developed a program called the "St. Pius X Institute of Adult Education and Catechetics." This project drew on the skills of many people, among them Monsignor Langenhorst, Father Breedlove, Father Baltasar

Monsignor Wolf and Father Hoover are shown with Miss Lucy Griffin, catechist, and the 1961 First Communion class. Altar boys are Rufino Mendoza, Jr., George Mendoza, and Florentino Cortez.
Photo courtesy of St. Patrick Cathedral Archives.

Pictured with Bishop Gorman are Father Eugene Witkowski, native son of St. Patrick's Parish; Father Edwin Ryan, whose first assignment was as assistant pastor at St. Patrick's; and Father William Hoover, assistant from 1960 to 1962, who returned as pastor in 1987.
Photo courtesy of St. Patrick Cathedral Archives.

Father Joseph Nagy, an assistant pastor in the 1950's.
Photo courtesy of St. Patrick Cathedral Archives.

Father J. Patrick Hazel served as assistant to Monsignors Wolf, DeFalco and Erbrick. He did pioneer work as Western Division director of the CCD.
Photo courtesy of St. Patrick Cathedral Archives.

Father Sam Metzger, an assistant to Monsignor Wolf.
Photo courtesy of Estelle Metzger.

Szarka, O. Cist., Dr. Frank Reuter of T.C.U., and others to present an area-wide program of adult education and catechetical formation. Hundreds attended. The program also used the facilities of Our Lady of Victory and St. Joseph's Hospital.

The same ecumenical spirit with its impulse to reach out to the spiritually hungry prompted Monsignor Wolf to establish a "Soul Clinic" offering instruction and counseling. A sign advertising the Soul Clinic stood in front of St. Patrick's rectory for a long time. It also led to the beginning of a weekly novena to "Our Lady of Return." The focal point of the novena was the icon of the Blessed Virgin at the summit of the reredos of the Marian altar. Each Saturday morning the novena prayers were said at that altar, pleading for the return of the lost and the unity of Christians.

****

The St. Ignatius building had been purchased from the Sisters of St. Mary, but the school which it housed could not be saved. Monsignor Wolf, having acquired the property for the parish, renamed the school "St. Patrick's Co-Cathedral Academy." It continued to operate under that title for a few years. The building was usable, but barely so. The resources of the parish were stretched to the limit by the purchase and by the renovation project. The enrollment had been declining for a decade. In 1950 there were 218 students; in 1955, 189. By the school year 1960-61 the enrollment stood at 105. Most of the students were parishioners, although some came from other parishes. The school was tuition-free, but that was not sufficient incentive to bring up the attendance. The parish itself had grown older, and the downtown school was not attractive to most of the younger families who lived at a distance.

In the 1960-61 school year, one sister of St. Mary commuted from O.L.V. to teach the first and second grades. Mrs. Jean Jasper taught the third and fourth, and Peggy Faught the fifth and sixth. The two highest grades were under Larry Phillips, helped by the assistant priests who were in and out teaching religion, history, and Spanish. The parish secretary, Jennie Hereford, also helped.

The closing of the school brought to an end 80 years of Catholic school education at the site. In the early 1960's, Catholic schools were still being built, but what happened at St. Patrick's would happen at many other places in the decades to come.

Her hands are raised in supplication: the Child rests upon her heart. The icon is richly ornamented and precious. Such images were venerated by Christians of the East for centuries. The art form has its own rules and accepted symbolism. The inscription reads "The Child of Knowledge."
Photo courtesy of St. Patrick Cathedral Archives.

Monsignor Wolf gave the invocation at breakfast on the last day of President John F. Kennedy's life.
Photo courtesy of St. Patrick Cathedral Archives.

65

ST. IGNATIUS

Three sisters of St. Mary of Namur arrived in Fort Worth on September 3, 1885, from St. Xavier's Academy, Denison, Texas. They had come at the invitation of Bishop Gallagher of Galveston to establish the fifth school of their mission in Texas. Led by Sister Anastasia as the first superior, Sister Claire and Sister Patricia moved into the Thomas Roche house located slightly south of the present day rectory, at that time the site of St. Stanislaus Church. They also began readying the Jacob Smith house, south of the Roche house, as a schoolhouse.

The order had already received a charter from the State of Texas on August 20, 1885, to operate St. Ignatius Academy. About that time Sister Anastasia had come to Fort Worth to purchase the two houses facing Throckmorton Street. After the two sisters had moved into the Roche house, Sister Anastasia returned to Denison to bring to Fort Worth two more sisters, Sister Adolphine and Sister Camilla, and a lay teacher, Miss Mollie Kirby. This was the first faculty of St. Ignatius.

The sisters had come to Fort Worth reluctantly, knowing that founding a new Catholic school in the frontier town of about 10,000 residents would not be easy. A major conflict existed due to the presence of another religious community, the Sisters of Mercy, who had maintained a school here since at least 1881. The Fort Worth City Directory of 1883-1884 lists St. Joseph Convent, a boarding and day school for young ladies, and St. Stanislaus Parochial School, a day school for boys and girls, both under the charge of the Sisters of Mercy, with Sister Theresa as the mother superior. Memories recorded later mention a school on Penn Street that remained active until 1887.

This community had existed here unofficially, ecclesiastically speaking, since the membership was made of up sisters who had previously abandoned other orders. They had come to Fort Worth, possibly from St. Louis, during the period between Bishop Dubuis' resignation and Bishop Gallagher's consecration. They had been asked to leave by the Bishop, but had refused to go. Only

after Sister Anastasia had received counsel and permission from her own Mother General in Belgium, did the Sisters of St. Mary agree to come to Fort Worth.

Obviously, such a small town, chiefly Protestant in make-up, could hardly support two Catholic academies, and the Sisters of St. Mary had little hope of acquiring many pupils. Their doubts proved groundless, however. At the opening of classes September 15, 1885, they counted 29 students. At the opening of the January term the school had 50 students. Several of these were boarders.

Many adjectives come to mind when reading the diaries and minutes of trustee meetings from the early days of St. Ignatius. The sisters seemed imbued with fierce determination to succeed, to build something of worth and endurance. Clear thinking, deliberate goals, an uncanny familiarity with finance, and steady confidence are among the impressions from their records.

Besides holding classes in the Smith house, the sisters continued St. Stanislaus School which had existed in the church since the days of Father Loughrey. Physical attributes of the building were not ideal for a school. A heavy curtain was used to separate the sanctuary from the class area. A fence was built between the buildings within months, presumably for privacy. By 1887 the sisters had bought two lots facing Jennings Avenue for a playground.

In November, 1888, the sisters agreed they needed to build "a new and strong building, of brick or stone, with modern improvements." The new building would stand in the middle of the lot 75 feet from Jennings and 120 feet from Throckmorton. A loan of $50,000

St. Ignatius School seen from the corner of Jennings and Twelfth.
Photo courtesy of Mrs. Polly Davidson.

was secured from Wiegman's Bank in Amsterdam. They selected J. J. Kane to serve as architect and superintendent of work. Kane (1822-1901) had come to Fort Worth in the mid-1870's from Washington, D.C., becoming a prominent architect here and throughout Texas. He served as president of the State Association of Architects, as well as the local association. The four-story limestone building he designed is a "simplified version of French Second Empire style, characterized by the mansard roof, dormer windows, cupola tower, decorative chimneys, and a tendency toward verticality." Today, St. Ignatius is the only building of this style and period surviving in Fort Worth.

From its inception, the main goal of St. Ignatius Academy was to provide a pervasive Catholic environment stressing the learning of Christian doctrine and the daily practice of the faith. The curriculum in 1885 included the four R's (reading, writing, arithmetic, and religion), etiquette, music, elocution, and calisthenics. Good penmanship of the Palmer Method was rewarded with certificates. Math was taught with an abacus held in the hand of the teacher and another larger one that stood on the floor. "Mental" math skills were practiced daily at random, for example, while distributing the cloaks. At first, slates were used for writing. Later, pencil tablets were distributed to be used completely before new ones could be issued.

To maintain discipline, the sisters used small wooden instruments, signals, brought from Belgium in the 1860's. Upon hearing its clicking sound, hundreds of students have become silent, sat up straighter, turned, opened books, started exams, gotten into line, genuflected, and given complete attention and authority to the holder of the signal.

High school classes of young

The chapel of St. Ignatius School was located on the first floor on the north side of the building.
Photo courtesy of St. Patrick Cathedral Archives.

women graduated from 1904-1910. Besides the regular academic classes, they studied geography, mythology, astronomy, and etymology. Recitals and the graduation exercises provided opportunity for the school to show off to the community the musical and dramatic talent of the students. Performances held in public theaters, such as the Byers Opera House, received great notice in the local newspapers of the day. Several of the sisters provided music classes in piano, violin, and voice and were considered among the best instructors in the city. Among them were Sister Philomena, Sister Clement, and Sister Mary Albertine.

By 1900 there were 30 boarders from Indian territory, Brownwood, Stephenville, and west Texas. Since the grounds did not provide sufficient area for exercise, the boarders would go on daily outings "into the town," out to St. Mary's

Sister Mary Albertine, S.S.M.N., (Theresa Duross), a native daughter of St. Patrick's Parish, entered the order in 1910.
Photo courtesy of St. Patrick Cathedral Archives.

Grove, and even as far as Arlington Heights. They would walk in rows of twos, always accompanied by a sister in the lead and another at the end.

Notes from the early journals tell of the growth and maintenance of the school. An iron fence was built on Throckmorton and Jennings in 1889. A motion was made to install a hot water heating system for the new building, not to exceed $1,500. Galleries to connect the new building with the two older houses were built. The yard on Jennings was graded and planted in 1890. A small, frame building behind the Roche house was built in 1891 for trunks and clothing of boarders and teachers. A playground, St. Mary's Grove, some distance from the school on the south side was purchased for $3,800 in 1895. St. Stanislaus Hall was adapted at this time to be the school for boys. It continued at this site until it was razed in 1908 to make room for the rectory.

By 1905 the school had increased in size to require the addition of an adjoining building constructed at a right angle to the original structure. About this time the sisters sold St. Mary's Grove and began plans to establish the "Annex," a mission school at Hattie Street and Kentucky Avenue that would later be Holy Name School. Expansion of the city around St. Ignatius caused the sisters to buy 26 acres on Hemphill Street in 1908 to build a large new school (Our Lady of Victory, 1910). In 1926 traffic demands from a modern city required the opening of 12th Street between Throckmorton and Jennings. To accomplish this, the school sold the land occupied by the addition. It was torn down along with the Roche house which had served as the music department for years.

Stability reigned at St. Ignatius throughout the war years and the Depression years. Then, when new parishes in the suburbs were established following World War II, enrollment fell so that plans were discussed to tear down the "old-fashioned" building and replace it with a modern facility which would attract new students and also serve as a much-needed parish hall. Fortunately, these plans were never realized. By the mid-1960's, local preservationists had requested the Amon G. Carter Foundation to fund a research project conducted by D. Blake Alexander of the University of Texas at Austin. Alexander designated fourteen buildings of the late 19th and early 20th century to be of such architectural and historical significance to Fort Worth's cultural heritage as to merit restoration and preservation. St. Ignatius and its neighbor, St. Patrick's, were two of the fourteen.

This building which opened in 1905 enabled St. Ignatius to expand to more than 400 pupils. It was torn down in 1926 to allow the city to open Twelfth Street between Throckmorton and Jennings. *Photo courtesy of* **The Texas Catholic.**

Taken from Throckmorton Street, this photo shows the faculty and students of St. Ignatius in the golden age of the school. *Photo courtesy of Lillian Simons.*

In October, 1956, Bishop Thomas Gorman purchased St. Ignatius Academy from the Sisters of St. Mary of Namur. The school continued as an elementary school until 1962. Several innovative attempts were made to bring more use to the building. An after school child-care program was initiated in 1960 for the children of people working in the downtown area. It was open to Catholic and Protestant students. Special classes in foreign languages, fine arts, and first aid were offered. The Texas Boys Choir used the building for several years as a rehearsal hall. Trinity Valley School, a private boys' school that grew out of the Boys Choir, began in a single classroom in St. Ignatius in 1959 with four students.

Since that time, St. Ignatius has enjoyed the distinction of being designated a Texas historical landmark and receiving an historical medallion. It has been completely refurbished throughout, from Lehane Hall in the basement (previously the laundry and kitchen) to the upstairs. There the ceilings have been lowered. Offices and classrooms have been built where the chapel and dormitories were. Today, the St. Patrick School of Religion conducts classes on Sunday for approximately 550 students from pre-Kindergarten through twelfth grade. Choir rehearsals for the cathedral adult choir and the children's choir can be heard weekly. RCIA classes meet each Sunday in the music room. General instruction classes given by the pastor or visiting priests are held throughout the school year.

The sisters who built St. Ignatius in 1888 might be surprised at how the city has grown and changed around their school, but they would probably find the learning and religious atmosphere inside very exciting and gratifying. The hallways and classrooms are filled with mementos, statues, banners, and religious pictures collected throughout the many years since its founding. Today, everyone associated with the building is proud of what it stood for in the past and what a strong symbol of Catholic institutional learning it is in today's world.

An early group picture at St. Ignatius. The reflection of the church may be seen in the window to the right.
Photo courtesy of St. Patrick Cathedral Archives.

1945 graduates of St. Ignatius School with their pages. Top row (l. to r.) Joe Hall, Lawrence Breedlove, Joseph Schumaker and Albert Joseph Griffith. Middle row: Earl Bush, Lee Darrah, Sam Fitzgerald, and John Oppie. The girls are Jean Anne Tierney and Judith Parman.
Photo courtesy of St. Patrick Cathedral Archives.

CHOIR

St. Patrick's has always enjoyed ecclesiastical music befitting the imposing structure. Some of the fondest memories of this church are of the inspiring music emanating from the choir loft. The Cathedral has marvelous acoustics, and the history of the church is full of many moving musical performances. The hallmarks of the Cathedral's rich music history include the many musical "firsts" associated with this parish and church, the renowned composer who once served as its choirmaster, and the longevity of service of choirmasters and choir members.

It appears that St. Patrick's has always sponsored a choir. Indeed, before the present church was constructed, St. Stanislaus Kostka Church had a choir under the direction of Professor Otten. On October 29, 1876, the frontier town of Fort Worth was awed by the choir's rendition of *Peter's Mass in D* at the first High Mass ever celebrated in Fort Worth. A local newspaper reported that "... music was rendered as was never before in this city ..." The newspaper account continued, "[t]o make particular mention of the voices would be an invidious distinction, for each and every one, either in chorus or solo, more than fulfilled the expectations of even the connoisseurs present ..."

Throughout the history of the Cathedral, the choir has performed at most major spiritual events and has offered numerous concerts. For years the choir offered a special musical performance at noon on Good Friday. The church was always filled with parishioners and downtown office workers, many of whom were non-Catholic. In 1984 the choir moved this Easter concert to Palm Sunday evening.

The choir's other major musical performance occurs each year at Midnight Mass on Christmas Eve.

These solemn services are well attended.

In 1945 Monsignor O'Donohoe persuaded Amon Carter and the *Fort Worth Star-Telegram* to broadcast and telecast simultaneously that year's Midnight Mass on WBAP-820 Radio and WBAP-TV. It was the first Mass ever to be televised in the Southwest. This practice continued for more than twenty years.

The present organ of St. Patrick's is the third in the Cathedral's one hundred year history. During Monsignor Nolan's tenure as pastor, he commissioned Professor Lamb to prepare specifications of a new grander pipe organ. This, installed in 1913, was a Hook & Hastings tracker pipe organ, said to be the largest and finest in the Southwest. The organ had 1,268 pipes ranging in size from 1/2 inch to sixteen feet in length. The pipes standing above the choir loft at the rear of the present church are all that remain of this organ, as it fell into grave disrepair during the late 1960's. The present organ, an Allen Digital Computer Organ with 57 stops, was installed in December 1975, during Monsignor Wiewell's tenure as rector.

Much of the musical history of the Cathedral revolves around a gentle man from England who served as organist and choirmaster for 43 years, William J. Marsh. Bill Marsh took his place in the choir loft on New Year's Day, 1920, and served until 1963, when he retired because of failing health. While at St. Patrick's, Marsh gained a nationwide reputation for his compositions of sacred music. Marsh wrote more than 20 masses and numerous anthems and hymns. His *Centennial Mass,* written for the Texas Centennial of 1936, was sung by a choir of more than 3,000 voices in Dallas that year. Similarly, his *St. Louis the Crusader Mass* was

Robert J. Lamb, organist-choirmaster from 1895 to 1920.
Photo courtesy of St. Patrick Cathedral Archives.

William J. Marsh, organist-choirmaster from 1920 to 1963.
Photo courtesy of St. Patrick Cathedral Archives.

James D. Barros, organist-choirmaster from 1967 to the present.
Photo courtesy of St. Patrick Cathedral/ David Barros photographer.

performed by a choir of 5,000 male voices in Boston's Holy Name Cathedral.

Mr. Marsh also was recognized for his composition of secular music. It was his composition of *Texas, Our Texas* which was selected in 1929 as the official Texas state song.

Bill Marsh passed away in 1971 at the age of 90 leaving behind a rich musical legacy. Monsignor O'Donohoe once described Bill Marsh's music as ". . . always singable, dignified, useful, and never annoying." The present St. Patrick's choir agrees, as it annually performs works of Mr. Marsh.

There must be something addictive about music in our Cathedral, for many, in addition to Bill Marsh, have had lengthy periods of service to the musical liturgy of the church. The first organist and choirmaster, Professor Robert J. Lamb, served from 1895 to 1920. The present organist and choirmaster, James Barros, has been at St. Patrick's since August, 1967. In addition, several choir members were recently honored for more than twenty years' service in the choir.

It was Jim Barros who assumed the task of rebuilding the choir and musical program at the Cathedral following the retirement of Mr. Marsh. When Jim assumed his position, there were only eight choir members. That number stands at about 40 today. Through much hard work, Jim has built the musical program at the Cathedral to a point where the choir and organist consistently perform music as beautiful and inspiring as the building in which it is presented.

DAVID BARROS PHOTO

GEORGE JARA PHOTO

DAVID BARROS PHOTO

GEORGE JARA PHOTO

St. Caecelia, St. Peter, St. Louis of France, St. Elizabeth of Hungary.

A collection of
liturgical vessels and
devotional objects
acquired by purchase or
donation over the years.
Most of the items came
into the possession of
the Cathedral in the
1950s.

The large ciborium
with the handles is used
for the reposition of the
Blessed Sacrament on
Holy Thursday. To the
left of the large
ciborium are an incense
boat and a thurible. The
chalice with the ivory
figures on the node was
given to the Cathedral
by Bishop Cassata.

The Stations of the Cross were made in Livorno, Italy, and erected in St. Patrick's Church in 1929. In style they matched the Gothic side altars which were in the church until 1947.

The statue of St. Anthony of Padua was made in Mexico City. It was carved out of cedar wood and completely covered with heavy gold leaf. The statue was then painted and the decorative designs on the garments were delicately chiseled through the paint to show the underlying gold.

The altar of the Pietá is rich in symbolism. The seven lights around the statue represent the seven sorrows as do the swords piercing the heart at the base of the altar. Three roses at the top symbolize Mary as daughter of God the Father, mother of God the Son, and spouse of God the Holy Spirit.

The altar of the Crucified is surmounted by an ancient and realistically carved crucifix from the State of Puebla, Mexico. The aureola behind the cross bears the instruments of the passion of the Lord. The crucifix is aggregated to the miraculous crucifix of Esquipulas in Guatemala. The Crucified Lord of Esquipulas is the patron of Guatemala. The image there has been venerated for more than 400 years.

Visitors often inquire about the statue of St. Roche with his faithful dog. Roche was a pilgrim saint of the fourteenth century. He is invoked as a protector against plague and pestilence. His statue was placed in St. Patrick's in 1944 as a prayer for protection from the polio epidemics which raged in Texas in those years.

WINDOWS

The visitor to St. Patrick's Cathedral is aware of the windows before any other feature of the church. His or her first comment is inevitably on the splendor of the glass and the magnificent visual impression made by the windows, especially in the interior of the building. Old-time parishioners, as well, generally consider the stained glass the most beautiful of the church's many pleasing facets.

The art of stained glass is very ancient. By the time the art reached its apex in the late middle centuries of Christianity, the builders of churches were able to create virtual miracles of stone and glass and light. The windows served to lift the mind and heart of the believer to God, to penetrate even the unbelieving soul, and also to promote the teaching mission of the Church by their representations of God's heroes and scenes from His saving activity in our world. People who could not read the parable of the good shepherd or the account of Jesus walking on the sea could lift up their eyes and see the scenes as light shone through the crafted glass.

The windows in St. Patrick's Cathedral are easily divided into two groups. Some were made and installed around the time of the completion of the church in the 1890's. The others date from the 1920's until perhaps as late as 1954. The untrained eye can quickly distinguish between the earlier and later windows. The bright colors of the earlier group distinguish them from the later group in which blue and deep red are the predominant colors. The tympana of the earlier windows show an architectural design; those of the later windows feature a cross. In the early windows of the saints, the name of the pictured saint appears in the nimbus or halo. The earlier windows, whether they were manufactured in Germany or America, are of the Munich school.

Generally speaking, the figures portrayed in the windows are familiar to most Catholics. Some, however, are not; so let's make a brief tour starting with the symbols of the Blessed Sacrament in the half window above the sacristy door. Moving to the viewer's right, we see St. Ignatius of Loyola and the Immaculate Conception. The crucifixion window claims our attention not only for its beauty, but because it incorporates such rich symbolism. We see there the apocalyptic lamb which was slain, Christ's triumph over death, and the Church's prayer that the sacrifice of Calvary, renewed on her altars, be taken by the angels to God's altar in heaven. To the right of the crucifixion window are St. Joseph, St. Aloysius, and the patron of the church, St. Patrick. In pondering this selection of saints it needs to be remembered that Father Guyot was very close to the Jesuit order and at one time intended to become a Jesuit himself.

The windows on the north side of the church from front to back are: an angel in adoration, St. Anthony, St. Therese of Lisieux, St. Philomena, St. Rita, St. Raphael, and St. Christopher. Next comes a saint few people recognize. He is St. Oliver Plunkett, a martyred Irish archbishop, executed in England in the closing years of the seventeenth century. Then come St. Frances of Rome, St. Clare, St. Louis of France, and St. Elizabeth of Hungary. Unfortunately, the confessional hides the windows portraying the sacrifice of Isaac by Abraham and the Assumption of the Blessed Virgin.

The windows of the south wall, from front to back, show St. Michael, the Sacred Heart of Jesus, St. Anne, St. Margaret Mary, St. Catherine of Siena, St. Joan of Arc, and St. Charles Borromeo. Then comes a particularly beautiful window of St. Caecilia, one of the early ones; then, St. Pius X, St. Francis of Assisi, and St. Stanislaus Kostka, patron of the parish before the change of name. There is then a particularly beautiful window picturing St. Peter. The last two, the Immaculate Conception and Our Lady of the Rosary, are partly hidden by the confessional.

The small clerestory windows are of the Munich school, installed when the church was built. The large east, or "rose" window, as well as some of the smaller windows facing Throckmorton Street, are of American art glass of the 1890's, set in geometrical patterns and representing no topic. The racks of pipes which partly hide the rose window are ornamental rather than functional. Thought has been given to removing them so that window could have its full effect within the church. Attention should be paid to the tympana above the side front entrances. These also belong to the early period.

Some of the windows show considerable deterioration, and their restoration is an important parish priority. The iron grillwork covering the windows was added to protect them after air-conditioning when it was no longer necessary for the windows to swing open. Many think that they detract from the windows by blocking the entry of light and that the windows could be well protected without them. Others consider the grills an enhancement because of the contrast with the whitewashed stone. The matter has yet to be resolved.

Margaret Lehane was a person of sunny disposition, straightforward, pleasant, and cheerful—usually. The one thing that could make her less than happy on any given day was pilferage of the money boxes in the church. The coin boxes on the votive light stands were always being broken into, to Margaret's considerable annoyance. It was a cross she had borne for a long time, for she had been sacristan of St. Patrick's Church for the greater part of her adult life. On this particular day in 1963, she was in the seventieth year of that life. Well, maybe it would be necessary to keep the church locked during the day. Neither Margaret nor the priests wanted to do it, but the acts of vandalism were so frequent now that perhaps they had no choice.

Actually, Margaret Lehane was more than a sacristan. She was friend and confidant to two generations of priests and parishioners. Father Publius Xuereb was stationed briefly at St. Patrick's when he came to the United States from Malta. His English was somewhat uncertain and he was very nervous about his first preaching assignment at the cathedral. Meeting Margaret in the sacristy he jokingly asked her if she would be willing to preach for him. "I do all my preaching at home," she replied, "but I'd be glad to hear confessions for you." Utterly loyal, she was very hardworking and completely dedicated to the beautiful old church whose care had been her life's work. The church had been new when Margaret

Margaret Lehane, sacristan of St. Patrick's Church for more than 50 years. She lived in St. Patrick's parish all her life, 1894-1972.
Photo courtesy of St. Patrick Cathedral Archives.

Lehane was baptized in its font by Father Guyot on the 6th of June, 1894. She and the church had grown old together. Nothing of significance had ever taken place there of which she had not been a part. Margaret made her home with her sisters, Theresa and Dorothy, in the family house on Samuels Avenue, but she came to church each morning early and often returned home late. She had worked for and with Monsignor Nolan, Monsignor O'Donohoe, and Monsignor Wolf. But there was little question that the present pastor, Monsignor DeFalco, was her favorite of all the priests who had come and gone. Now he was leaving St. Patrick's, too, and forgetting the rifled votive stands, she felt a keen sense of loss. The date was April 17, 1963, and it had just been announced that Monsignor Lawrence DeFalco had been named Bishop of Amarillo by Pope John XXIII. Father Hazel had come to the sacristy to tell her the news.

He had only been pastor for a short while, having been appointed to the parish in January of 1962. Fourteen months wasn't enough time for a new pastor to make much of a start. But Father DeFalco had been at St. Patrick's before, and Margaret could remember the far off day in 1942 when he had come to the parish, newly ordained, to begin an eleven-year stay as an assistant priest. In that eleven years he had endeared himself to Margaret and to the whole parish by the simplicity and goodness of his life and the humility and charity which characterized his ministry. Well, now the Church had made him a bishop, and though Margaret approved of the choice, and no one could find fault with the poor, dying Pope, it would still be hard to see him go. There was a Council of the Church taking place in Rome, and she supposed the new bishop would be a part of it, but that seemed somewhat remote. The big thing now was to get the church ready for Bishop DeFalco's upcoming consecration. There would be a lot of work to do.

****

Father Lawrence DeFalco was a native of Pennsylvania—McKeesport, specifically. He came from a large, thoroughly Catholic family, the children of Ross DeFalco and Margaret Desmone DeFalco. He received his education for the priesthood at St. John's Home Mission Seminary in Little Rock, Arkansas, and was ordained in St. Andrew's Cathedral in Little Rock by Bishop John B. Morris on June 11,

CHAPTER 6

Shamrock Plans

1942. Two weeks later he came to St. Patrick's in Fort Worth to take up his first assignment. Eleven years, then and now, is a long time to be assistant pastor in one place, but the circumstances seemed to warrant it. His work was of such quality, and Monsignor O'Donohoe held him in such high regard, that any plan the aged Bishop Lynch might have had to move him was successfully forestalled. When Bishop Gorman finally insisted on moving him, Monsignor O'Donohoe wrote a letter to DeFalco's father in Pennsylvania which will serve as a summary of his achievement as assistant pastor:

"All of us here at St. Patrick's are deeply grieved, especially myself, over the changes that Bishop Gorman has seen fit to do. Of course, none of us want to oppose progress and promotion, but we have been so happy with your son and love him so much. We just can't help regret giving him up.

"For ten years he has been an integral part of my life. He has worked loyally and lovingly for the parish, the good of souls, and for God and has done so much good for all of us . . . . In the years he's been here, he's accomplished more and been responsible for more good than any other priest in the some 80 years of this parish's existence. Not only the parish but the city loves him and is sincerely grieved at his leaving us."

These are words of high praise. Bishop Gorman, though, also saw Father DeFalco's worth and wanted him for his curia.

From St. Patrick's Father DeFalco went first to Dallas, then to Chicago to observe the workings of the marriage tribunal there. In September of 1953 he was sent to Rome to study Canon Law at the Gregorian University. He came back to Dallas in 1955 with a licentiate degree in Church law. He was named secretary to the tribunal of the Diocese of Dallas-Fort Worth, an office which he held until his return to St.

St. Patrick's CCD executive board in 1962. Members, front row, left to right, are: Mrs. Glen Hinz, Mrs. Tommy Farrell, Miss Frances Oechsner, Miss Helen Barnes, Mrs. Joseph Bandor and Mrs. Chester Hollis. Back row, left to right: John Wilson, Maurice Chiasson, Joseph Meyers, Frank Ivory, Robert Cain and Rufino Mendoza. *Photo courtesy of Mrs. Eileen Farrell.*

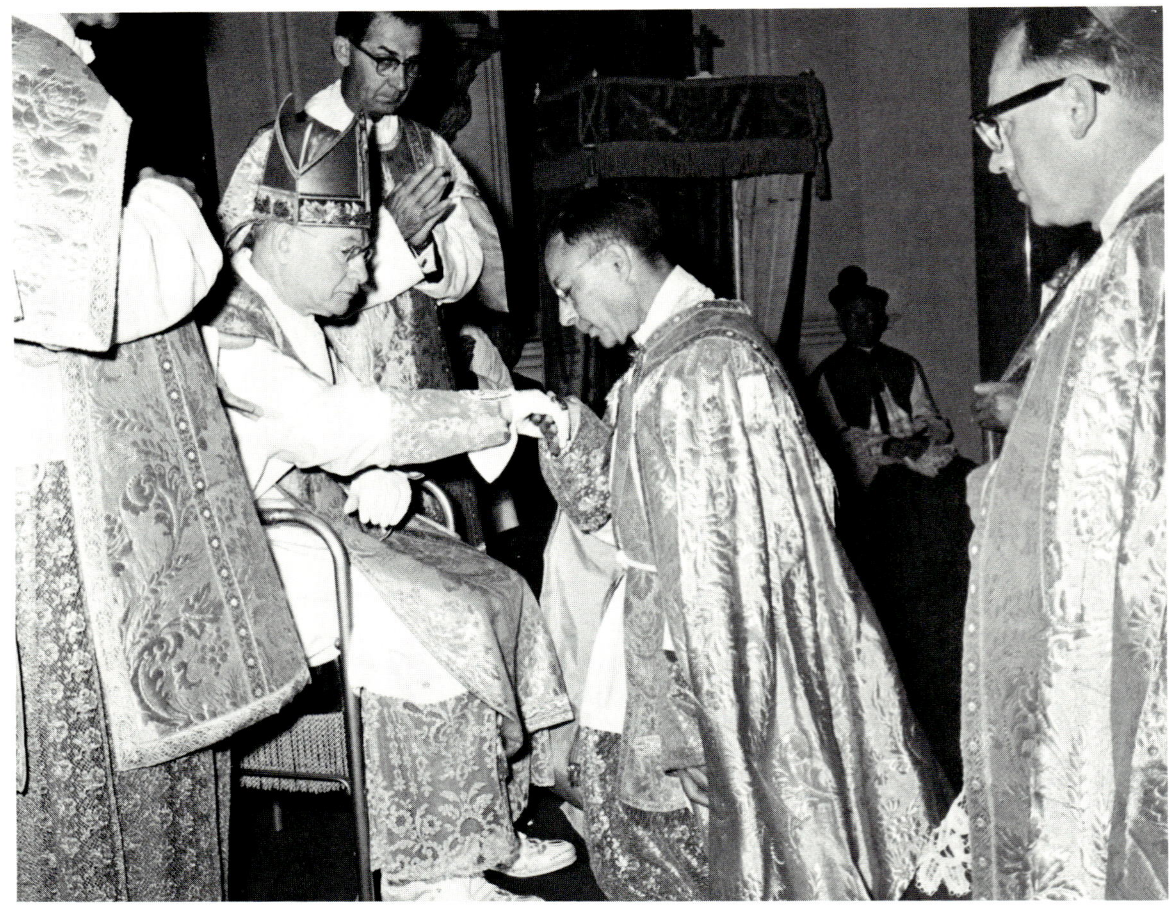

Patrick's as pastor in January of 1962. During his years in the Chancery Office in Dallas he was, for a brief time, administrator of St. Michael's Parish in McKinney and served for six years as pastor of the parish of Our Lady of Perpetual Help in Dallas. Such, in brief, was the life story of the newly appointed bishop.

The consecration of the new bishop was quickly arranged. It took place in St. Patrick's Co-Cathedral. Bishop Gorman was the consecrating bishop assisted by Bishop Albert Fletcher of Little Rock and Bishop Joseph Green of Lansing, Michigan, a fellow student of DeFalco's in Rome. Margaret Lehane sat in a place of honor. It was the only episcopal consecration held in St. Patrick's in its century of years. The preacher of the occasion, Father Edwin Johnson, a seminary classmate, evoked the memory of Monsignor O'Donohoe.

"Could we hear his words," Father Johnson said, "I am sure we would hear, 'I knew it from the start.' If there are bells in heaven, he is ringing them today . . . ."

Bishop DeFalco served the Church of Amarillo for sixteen years. He did go to the Council in Rome where he favored many of the conciliar reforms, especially the modification of the Mass to permit the use of English or the mother tongue of each place.

He died on September 22, 1979, in Amarillo where, as in Fort Worth, his memory is cherished and his name held in honor.

The historian of twenty-five years later who searches both the records of the church and the memories of the parishioners sees no renovations wrought or statues installed by him. But those who remember him speak of charity dispensed, of converts made, of shattered lives and broken families put back together, of level-headed advice given, of hard, selfless work and of steadiness of faith and purpose.

****

The bells of St. Patrick's Co-Cathedral began to toll at precisely 9:30 on the morning of April 8, 1968. Monsignor Joseph Erbrick, the pastor, had announced that the bell would be struck exactly 39 times in memory of the 39-year-old civil rights leader, Martin Luther King, whose funeral services were beginning at the same time in Atlanta, Georgia. Monsignor Erbrick, whose pastorate spanned the middle years of the turbulent 1960's, was aware of the transformation going on in American life and wanted St. Patrick's to meet the new developments with an effective program of ministry.

Apart from what was happening in the world at large, the changes taking place in the immediate neighborhood of the Co-Cathedral were truly epic. The city had plans for a municipal complex which would involve the re-routing of Texas Street and the clearing of the blocks on the west side of Jennings from Tenth Street all the way to Lancaster Avenue. They were going to build a new city hall, an office building, and clear an extensive area for parking. In front of the church a whole section of the city was slated to disappear. Tenth, Eleventh, and Twelfth Streets were to be closed from Houston to Commerce, and fourteen whole blocks of downtown Fort Worth were to be leveled to make room for a convention center and necessary parking facilities. St. Patrick's property was going to be affected by all this renovation. The city had a master plan for routing traffic into the convention center area. It would allow Texas Street to lead into Twelfth Street which, in turn, would bend through St. Ignatius' front yard so that traffic could move easily onto Throckmorton Street going north.

It was a vast change in the whole picture of downtown. In the interval before the new center was built, it was possible, from St. Ignatius' front porch, to look east at the entrance to the Santa Fe depot five block away. The whole part of the city that had existed between the two was gone.

Quite apart from what the city was doing, St. Patrick's had problems of its own. Monsignor Erbrick felt the need to offer better and more varied services to the parishioners and to the community, but the facilities at St. Patrick's were plainly inadequate for such an expansion of activities. Besides that, there was a considerable debt. The church and rectory had been magnificently renovated, but that had been costly. On top of it, a lot of money had been needed to acquire the St. Ignatius

property from the Sisters of St. Mary. If that were not enough, it was a sad fact that the Diocesan Educational Development drive for the building of high schools had fallen far short of raising the necessary funds for completing the schools. The parishes had been assessed to make up the deficit, and the share assigned to St. Patrick's was substantial. Besides these weighty obligations, the parishes had been taxed again to help with the construction of the new Holy Trinity Seminary in Dallas. Everyone was glad that these things had been done, but it made it difficult for many parishes to contemplate costly improvements on their own grounds. The parish had, indeed, acquired the St. Ignatius Building, but it was questionable that it could be considered an asset. It looked fine from the street, but inside it was a sorry spectacle. And people were inclined to doubt that much could be done with it. Monsignor Erbrick had two expert groups check it out, and both agreed that to make it safe and usable for the purposes of the parish would be prohibitively costly. In fact, the building was renovated in later years and made to serve some of the parish needs, but anyone who remembers the building at its worst, as this author does, can sympathize with the pessimism of Monsignor Erbrick's advisors.

A finance committee was formed to take a hard look at the monetary condition of the parish. The members were B. V. Haberer, John L. Lewis, Walt Connolly, and Clifford Taylor, auditor. The committee made the necessary projections based on parish income and parish obligations. Others studied the space needs. A new building was proposed which would contain not only classrooms, but offices, meeting areas, a choir room, a bride's room, a lot of storage space, and a downtown Catholic information center. St. Patrick's parishioners were invited to give their suggestions by way of a parishwide survey. They brought forth a wealth of ideas. The information center was highly popular. Suggestions were made as to several kinds of adult education, including literacy programs. Facilities were thought to be needed for youth and athletic programs and for day care for children of working mothers.

Based on all this data a program of development known as the "Shamrock Plan" was drawn up and presented to the parishioners. It involved debt reduction, the meeting of current responsibilities, and the eventual building of a new facility with the 100th anniversary year of 1970 as a target. Much of it happened. The program of debt reduction was very successful. Many of the desired programs were carried out in the existing facilities. The building, of course, was not built. Monsignor Erbrick's term was cut short by changes altogether unforeseen. By 1970 there was not only a new pastor, but a new bishop and a new diocese, and, with these developments, a whole new set of priorities.

The Shamrock Plan called for a multi-purpose building to replace St. Ignatius. *Photo courtesy of St. Patrick Cathedral Archives.*

Father Joe Erbrick was no stranger to Fort Worth when he came to St. Patrick's. The early years of his priesthood were spent at All Saints Church on the North Side where he is still remembered after all these years. He had been involved with the establishment of St. Peter's and St. Paul's parishes in the years after the war. He had served also as pastor of the venerable Holy Name parish on the southeast side of town. He was probably the best-known Catholic priest in Fort Worth in those years. Many of his goals at St. Patrick's were achieved. The church became a center of ecumenism in the city, joining the Fort Worth Council of Churches in 1967. Sacred music was restored to an important place in the Co-Cathedral. Under Erbrick's guidance the Catholic Chorale, composed of Catholic high school students from public and private schools, was formed and well received. The very significant Cathedral Classics Seminars were established. These seminars provided citizens of all faiths an opportunity to study theology and the classics under the guidance of scholars from the University of Dallas. The life of the parish and of the community was greatly enriched by these achievements.

****

A spot check of parish bulletins in the 1960's tells a lot about the life of the parish. Much of it was the same as, and much of it different from, the present. In those days the bulletin was called "The Shamrock." It was usually printed in green ink. In 1960 Father William Hoover and Father Patrick Hazel were listed as assistants. The CYO was selling greeting cards. A regular second collection was taken up for a free parochial school. CCD classes were held on Saturdays. Mmes. M. U. Claiborne, J. Lee Johnson, Jr., Lillian Simons, E. D. Tuttle, and H. J. Rudloff had the altar assignment, and a "silver polishing party" was scheduled for 9:00 a.m. on Tuesday, December 6, 1960. In the bulletins of 1967, we read that the Sunday Masses were scheduled at 6:00, 7:00, 8:00, 9:30, 11:00, 12:15, and 5:10. The daily Masses were at 6:45, 8:00, and 12:00 noon. Father Patrick Lynch and Father Michael Xuereb were the assistants, and Father Joseph Kopczewski and Father John Donnelly were in residence. The Mass attendance on an average Sunday was 2,180 (slightly less than 1988), and the weekly collection averaged $1,760. "The Shamrock" pointed out that this offering represented 80¢ per person. Easter attendance that year, however, had been 3,462, and the offering of $3,012.50 was 90¢ per person attending. Father Lynch was giving a Monday night series of lectures on Catholicism which all might attend without obligation. Discussion clubs were active in the parish. Jim Davidson was the co-ordinator. Parking was a problem, and people were severely warned about blocking the driveways—certainly, this is a constant in the history of the parish.

Bulletins of 1964 tell of a challenge from the CYO basketball team to the adults of the parish. Adults who wanted to play might call Emma Sweet or Dominic Rappich. Altar boy assignments reveal that among the active servers was E. R. Kuelthau at the early Mass. Other names are those of the Circe brothers, John Wilson, Doyle Wood, Tim Farrel, Bill Parker, M. Touchon, Dennis Blaschke, Drew Womack; Rufino, George, and David Mendoza, James Davidson, George Sandoval, Jack Powell, David Mills, and J. Sawey. It was stressed, for some reason, that altar boys were not to wear white socks. Some of the ladies attending to the altars were Mmes. L. D. Hopkins, W. P. Curtin, E. G. Kuelthau, Fred Guminski, Dave Elias, A. J. Gilstrap, Jr., and E. A. Schiffers. The St. Vincent de Paul Society met on Tuesdays at 7:00 p.m., and the Legion of Mary on Wednesdays at 5:15 p.m. Novenas to St. Jude and Our Lady of Return were held on Sunday evening and Saturday morning. Fathers Pat Hazel, Michael Flanagan, and William Vonk were the assistant pastors, and many of the weekday Masses were being offered for the happy repose of John F. Kennedy.

There was an active CYO in the mid-sixties which met in the "Shamrock Room" (basement of the church). St. Patrick's had a complete CCD board as required by the diocese. The Apostles of Good Will served coffee and rolls after the Sunday Masses. A parish mission was given most years. In 1964 a Father MacMahon was the preacher.

****

The June 29, 1968, issue of *The Texas Catholic* carried a couple of items of historic interest to Fort Worth Catholics. Court Louise of the Catholic Daughters of America held its last meeting at St. Ann's Club on Penn Street. The club, a businesswomen's residence for forty years, located first on Fifth Street and then moved to the Penn Street location in 1929, thus passed into history. The building was to be torn down.

That same week Fathers Eugene Witkowski, Joseph Scantlin, and Joseph Schumacher concelebrated a Mass at Worth Ranch on the Brazos River to dedicate a campsite in honor of John Edward Gillespie, who was retiring after 41 years service as scoutmaster of Troop 32, sponsored by K. of C. Council 759.

These items were on the back pages. The front page of the paper was dominated by the news of the new pastor of St. Patrick's. Newly consecrated Bishop John J. Cassata was coming to Fort Worth in a dual role as auxiliary bishop and pastor of the Co-Cathedral in Fort Worth.

****

"In the name of myself, the clergy, the religious, and the people of the Diocese of Dallas-Fort Worth, I receive with open arms our newly consecrated bishop." These words were part of Bishop Gorman's homily as he welcomed Bishop John J. Cassata to the diocese.

It was June 26, 1968. The following day Bishop Cassata came to Fort Worth to be installed as pastor of St. Patrick's and celebrated Mass for the first time at the altar of the Co-Cathedral. Priests of the various religious orders serving in the diocese were concelebrants. Father Patrick Lynch and Father Richard Weaver co-ordinated the ceremonies of the Mass. A civic reception followed at the Texas Hotel with Mayor DeWitt McKinley and Beeman Fisher of the Chamber of Commerce extending the city's welcome. Prayers were offered by Rabbi Robert J. Shurr and by the Right Reverend William Paul Barnes, the resident suffragan bishop of the Episcopal Church. Thus St. Patrick's received its seventh pastor.

Although Bishop Cassata's pastorate was of short duration, ending when Fort Worth became a separate diocese with Bishop Cassata as its first bishop, as Ordinary of the new diocese he made St. Patrick's the center for the administration of the new see. Necessary alterations were made in the lower level of the cathedral rectory, and it served for more than a decade as the chancery office of Fort Worth. From there Bishop Cassata directed the early growth of the diocese and carefully laid the foundations on which its future would be built.

The center room on the south side of the rectory was used for reception since the main entrance to the office was there, facing the church. The large north front room served as an office for the chancellor and the Bishop's secretary, Phyllis Constantine. Both the early chancellors of the diocese, Monsignor Eugene Witkowski and Father Dan Williams, were residents of the cathedral rectory. The south front room was Bishop Cassata's own office. The south center room housed the financial records office of Mrs. Tyree Grimes. The large room at the back of the house was the office of the marriage tribunal. This arrangement lasted until Bishop Delaney arrived, when the administrative offices were moved to temporary quarters on Bolt Street near Seminary South. Eventually, all diocesan offices were brought together in the new Catholic Center on the west side of the city which was completed in 1985.

The Diocese of Fort Worth was formally established on October 21, 1969, at 4:00 p.m. in St. Patrick's Cathedral, which was filled to capacity. Monsignor Vincent J. Wolf, a former

pastor, as representative of the clergy, greeted the Apostolic Delegate, Archbishop Luigi Raimondi, and presented the "Letter of Establishment" to him, together with the "Executorial Decree." These documents, as well as the letters of the Bishop's appointment, were read to the assembled crowd by Father Joseph Schumacher. Bishop Cassata was then led to the *cathedra,* the episcopal chair, and presented with his crozier. Representatives of the clergy, religious, and laity then approached the new Bishop to offer their allegiance and their obedience. Archbishop Raimondi was then chief concelebrant at a Mass at which all the bishops of Texas were concelebrants. Bishop Cassata read the Gospel and delivered the homily, during which he expressed satisfaction over the more than a year he had spent in Fort Worth as pastor of St. Patrick's. "These have been fleeting and happy months. As I now scan the faces before me, I see many familiar ones. I do not feel the loneliness of a stranger; there is no quiver in my voice, no feeling of trepidation. I know that I have been accepted here with fraternal cordiality and an intimacy far beyond any expectation I had prayed for. My words of profound gratitude at this moment are, at best, inadequate to each of you . . . ."

It was a great moment. Co-Cathedral no longer, St. Patrick's would henceforth be called simply "The Cathedral." The old church was adequate to the honor. Father Guyot had known what he was doing.

1970 was a centennial year for the parish. The long-accepted date for its establishment was 1870 when Mass began to be celebrated on a regular basis in the small city of Fort Worth. Since no special month or day was associated with that long-ago event, it was decided to celebrate the anniversary on the patronal feast of the parish, St. Patrick's Day. The church was full. The choir sang, and the list of priests and bishops involved in the anniversary Mass included many names of those who had made recent parish history. Bishop Cassata of Fort Worth was the principal celebrant. Joining him at the altar were Bishop Thomas Tschoepe, once an assistant at St. Patrick's, Bishop Lawrence DeFalco, a former assistant and pastor, the retired Bishop Gorman, and Bishop Augustine Danglmayr. Monsignor Erbrick and Monsignor Wolf were also among the concelebrants. Bishop DeFalco preached and honored the feast day by recalling the faith of the Irish pioneers of the last century who had built the church here on the foundations laid by the Spanish and French missionaries.

Monsignor William McCoey made the final arrangements for the centennial celebration. He had received his appointment as pastor of St. Patrick's only a month before. It is interesting to note that the first three pastorates, Guyot's, Nolan's, and O'Donohoe's, had spanned 72 years. Now, in only 14 years, five different pastors had been appointed. If continuity suffered, however, there were compensations. Each of the five brought distinctive gifts to the task. Each added luster to the old church and strengthened the faith of the parish community. It is also interesting to note that Monsignor McCoey was the third Pennsylvania-born priest to serve as pastor, equaling, in fact, the number born in Texas. McCoey was born in Philadelphia in 1920 and was educated for the priesthood at St. John's Home Mission Seminary in Little Rock, Arkansas. That seminary and the state of Pennsylvania both made vital contributions to

Monsignor William J. McCoey, founder of St. John's Parish, Fort Worth, came to St. Patrick's in 1970. *Photo courtesy of Mrs. Edith Hardwick.*

the ranks of the clergy of Fort Worth and Dallas during the middle years of this century.

Monsignor McCoey had held several important pastorates in the diocese before coming to St. Patrick's. Most recently he had organized St. John's Parish in North Richland Hills and had directed the construction of the school and the spacious church on Glenview Drive. The high point of Monsignor's life came with his years of service to the Confraternity of Christian Doctrine. He was diocesan CCD director for Dallas-Fort Worth and also associate director of the National Center of the CCD in Washington, D. C. He was a key figure in planning and chairing the great National and Inter-American CCD Congress in Dallas in late November of 1961. This Congress, presided over by the Papal Secretary of State, Cardinal Cicognani, was certainly the grandest event ever held under Catholic auspices in this area.

Monsignor McCoey is remembered by the parishioners as a gentle and considerate person, always appreciative of anything done for him or for the parish. The Sunday Mass schedule was substantially unchanged at that time, but weekday Masses were now two in number, at 6:45 a.m. and 12:05 p.m. Priests at St. Patrick's were also responsible for the daily Mass at the Carmelite Monastery on Sunset Terrace. This responsibility rested with the Cathedral from 1964 until the sisters moved to their new monastery in Arlington in the mid-1980's. Usually, one of the priests in residence would say the Mass. Father Eugene Witkowski and Father Joseph Carlin, S.J., were the residents.

Father Witkowski was chancellor of the diocese, and Father Carlin was connected with Catholic Charities. Father Thomas Taaffe also lived at St. Patrick's and helped as he was able until his death in January of 1978. Father John Donnelly was the assistant until he asked for retirement in midsummer of 1972. His place was taken by Father Reginald Kelly. Margaret Lehane died in September of 1972, and Martin Baskin, who had assisted her, took over as sacristan. Parishioners of that time also gratefully remember Fred Guminski, who for so many years opened the church for the early Mass.

A significant event of 1972 was the renovation of the lower level of the St. Ignatius Building. The staircase leading up to the first floor was removed, thus opening up the whole spacious area. The Carter Foundation generously made the renovation possible and saw the project through to completion. The beautiful new hall was dedicated to the memory of Margaret Lehane. It remains "Lehane Hall" to this day.

The pastor was very interested in the music program and envisioned a pipe organ for the church. He also arranged occasional mariachi Masses and mañanitas which were held at 4:30 in the morning.

There was a weekly Mass attended by the hearing-impaired and signed by Mrs. Eileen Farrell. This continued for more than a decade. Eventually it was moved to All Saints. The Cursillistas of Fort Worth had occasional inter-parochial Ultreyas at St. Patrick's, and there was a flourishing Cursillo group in the parish.

The Altar Society was quite active in the early 1970's. They conducted a bake sale each month on the front porch of the rectory. Names appearing in the records in connection with this project are: Mmes. Mildred Bandor, W. K. Stripling III, DeWitt Condit, E. D. Tuttle, L. D. Hopkins, Walter Bennett, L. A. Blaschke, O. R. Pitts, Berlu Cabral, Agnes Unsworth, Corrine Gathings, and Malinda Rhodes.

Also active were Misses Vivian Eikhoff, Margaret Dunn, Lucy Griffin, Ramona Martinez, Mrs. Lorenza Hartnibbsrig, and Mrs. Ethel Tillery.

Also Mmes. Lola Escalante, Joseph Cruz, Felipe Navejar, Kenneth Davis, Walter Black, John Malcolm, T. C. Bartula, A. H. Edens, and Mary Stephens.

The Legion of Mary and the St. Vincent de Paul Society were active at the time. It was at this time, also, that permission was secured to use the parking lot south of City Hall. Parishioners were asked to avail themselves of the privilege.

Monsignor McCoey was quite ill in the last months of 1972. Friends and parishioners prayed earnestly for his recovery. To the sorrow of the whole parish he died on February 4, 1973. He, by force of will, had remained as active as possible until the very end.

Top row: (l. to r.) Father Michael Irwin, Father William Vonk, Father Richard Weaver, Father Michael Flanagan. Bottom row: (l. to r.) Father Charles King, Father Wilfred DeFevere, Father Michael Xuereb, Father Patrick Lynch, Father Reginald Kelly. Photos courtesy of St. Patrick Cathedral Archives.

CATHEDRAL CLASSICS AND CHORALE

"If as many as 10 people sign up for 'The Influence of Dante's *Divine Comedy* upon Western Civilization,' we'll go ahead and sponsor it," said Monsignor Erbrick.

When registration had to be cut off at 70—mostly non-Catholic civic leaders—the first session of Cathedral Classics Seminars started with a bang. Professors were recruited from the University of Dallas, and they approached the subject from their different disciplines, so that the audience got not only the literary perspectives, but also philosophical, theological, historical, and psychological points of view. Grown-up students included Dr. May Owen, for whom a branch of Tarrant County Junior College is named; Stephen Seleny, founder and headmaster of Trinity Valley School; doctors and lawyers; public school teachers and Catholic school teachers; and one precocious high school student who, as a result of this course, won a statewide essay contest with his essay on Dante.

Then there was the cry for "More!" from the participants, who had found that, despite the fact that the majority of them had college degrees and graduate professional degrees, philosophy and theology had not been included among the subjects they studied.

"These professors make me feel so ignorant," lamented an architect's wife—an Episcopalian civic leader. One of her friends replied, "I suppose that realization is the beginning of a real learning process."

The next Cathedral Classics Seminar was built around three classic works: *The Iliad, The Aeneid,* and St. Augustine's *City of God,* and it was titled "Man and His City." Again, when the first 70 registered, the rest of the applicants had to be turned away. The seminars were conducted in St. Ignatius before the

restoration took place. It seemed amazing that such influential and mostly affluent people would come to such dismal, run-down headquarters and pay for the privilege.

They were, however, getting more than their money's worth. The Cistercian professors who spoke had studied at the great universities of Europe, and they gave a new depth to the meaning of adult education. People taking part in the seminars were given a reading list ahead of time, and study sheets were prepared for them.

The third Cathedral Classics Seminar was "Concepts of Virtue: Aristotle and Aquinas." Again, the influence of these philosophers upon drama, art, civilization, and religion was stressed by professors of philosophy, theology, and literature. Drs. Don and Louise Cowan, moving spirits of the University of Dallas in the '60's, added their zest to the scholarly presentation of the Cistercians and the Dominicans from the University of Dallas.

Dr. Felix Gwozdz, far left, and Monsignor Joseph Erbrick, far right, with Bishop Gorman and the Cathedral Chorale in the sanctuary of St. Patrick's Co-Cathedral. *Photo courtesy of Margaret Womack.*

The fourth Cathedral Classics Seminar was "Visions of Utopia: Plato, St. Thomas More, and Karl Marx." Included in these lectures were professors of political theory as well as the usual professors of literature, philosophy, theology, and science.

There were more seminars. Each group of lectures lasted for six weeks and was held at night. At the end, participants were invited to suggest and then to vote on the subjects for the next group of lectures.

****

Another fine project under Catholic auspices was begun when Dr. Felix Gwozdz, who had his master's degree in music as well as being a physician, said to Monsignor Joseph Erbrick, pastor of St. Patrick's Co-Cathedral, "I will direct a city-wide Catholic youth chorus if we can round up 30 high school students from public and Catholic schools.''

One Sunday afternoon in September, more than 30 high school students met at the home of Dr. and Mrs. Harry Womack, 1520 Thomas Place. Within fifteen minutes of their arrival, Dr. Gwozdz had the teenagers at work learning *Ave Verum.*

Dr. Gwozdz had a terrific sense of humor as well as a knowledge of music. He had a temper, along with his musical genius. He let it be known from the beginning that he would not stand for students' being absent or tardy to the 4 o'clock Sunday afternoon rehearsals. After the first rehearsal, sessions were held at the unrefurbished St. Ignatius School. Mrs. Margaret Womack was in charge of organization, Dr. Gwozdz of music, and Monsignor Erbrick had the veto power over everything. The Chorale sang at official church celebrations, especially in the Cathedral, but it also put on a yearly musical and an annual 30-minute Christmas television show.

A parent proclaimed: "My children got more culture from the experience of being in the Cathedral Chorale than from anything else in their teenage educational lives."

This rare picture of forked lightning over St. Patrick's Church was made by photographer Bob Abey in 1947.
Photo courtesy of The University of Texas at Arlington Libraries.

HISTORICAL RECOGNITION

The buildings—St. Patrick's Church, St. Ignatius, and the parish rectory—are among the oldest buildings in Fort Worth. The church, in particular, and St. Ignatius are of an architectural style that has disappeared. Ninety-nine percent of the buildings which stood in Fort Worth around 1890 have long since been demolished and replaced. It had to be that way because Fort Worth is a living city and not a museum. Nevertheless, it is of great importance to the whole community that buildings, representative of eras long gone, be preserved. A community must know its roots and cherish them. It is necessary that present and future be carefully integrated with the past. A city and its people must have an identity. That identity involves preserving significant features of the cityscape of long ago.

The church, likewise, is no museum; but the church, too, has a heritage, and that heritage is absolutely essential to her self-understanding and to the identity of her people. Both the church and the city have lived in history and are what they are because of that history. If the people of St. Patrick's and of the whole community do not carefully preserve what they have, then it is the future and the people of the future who will be the losers.

Recognition of the historic significance of the St. Patrick's complex of buildings began long ago. On December 2, 1962, the Texas State Historical Committee made a presentation of historic medallions to six buildings in the area. They were the Knights of Pythias Castle Hall at Third and Main Streets, St. Patrick's Cathedral, St. Ignatius Academy, the Van Zandt cottage on Crestline Road, the log cabins relocated in Forest Park, and Holy Comforter Episcopal Church in Cleburne. On hand to receive the medallion were Monsignor L. M. DeFalco and a group of parishioners. St. Patrick's and St. Ignatius as early as 1962 joined the select group of edifices which had achieved this recognition.

In June, 1971, Monsignor McCoey was notified that the Tarrant County Historical Survey Committee would present a descriptive metal plate to be affixed near the historical medallion. The plate was provided by the Junior League of Fort Worth. It contains a brief sketch of the building and some of its principal features.

Finally, in 1985, all three buildings were enrolled in the National Register of Historic Places. Appropriate plaques were affixed to all three buildings.

One step still needs to be taken. Before St. Patrick's was built, a frame church dedicated to St. Stanislaus stood on the property. For sixteen years it was the parish church. After 1892 the building was used as a parochial school for boys. The building stood until 1908 when it was demolished to make room for the present rectory. As the forerunner of St. Patrick's, St. Stanislaus is clearly an integral part of the history of the parish. No building remains to receive a medallion, but application has been made for an historical marker to be erected on the spot where the old church once stood. It is part of our past, and it must not be forgotten.

Monsignor Erbrick, Mrs. Walter Klein and Mr. Robert Cain examine the plaque presented to the Cathedral by the Texas Historical Survey.
Photo courtesy of **The Texas Catholic.**

Monsignor John M. Wiewell took up his charge as pastor of St. Patrick's Cathedral on Mother's Day, May 13, 1973, with the promise: "I shall give you the best that I have in spiritual and administrative leadership.... Humbly I ask for your prayers and co-operation." The words appeared in a pastoral message at the top of the bulletin, a little sermonette that would be a feature of the bulletin throughout Monsignor Wiewell's tenure. He had come to St. Patrick's after several years of service at Holy Name Parish in Fort Worth. As a young priest, the Oklahoma-born Wiewell had been secretary to Bishop Joseph P. Lynch. Later, having become pastor of St. Bernard's Parish in Dallas, he built the complete parish facility there—school, rectory, and a splendid church.

The same bulletin which offered Monsignor Wiewell's promise also carried the names of the new Altar Society officers: Mrs. John Malcolm, Mrs. Robert Turley, Mrs. Charles Tegethoff, Mrs. A. H. Edens, Mrs. Clarence Sawey, Miss Margaret Dunn, and Mrs. L. D. Hopkins. A survey of other parish bulletins for the summer and early fall of 1973 tells us what was going on at St. Patrick's in those days. The Third Order of St. Francis was meeting on the third Sunday of each month at 3:00 p.m., and the choir was rehearsing at 7:30 p.m. each Wednesday. The Altar Society was still conducting monthly bake sales. On June 17 Father Frank Uroda was welcomed to the parish staff, joining Father Kelly and Father Taaffe. In July a change was announced in the Sunday Mass schedule. The 7:15 and 8:30 a.m. Masses were to be combined into one Mass at 8:00, and the Saturday morning Mass was also to be at 8:00. James Barros was looking for instrumentalists to join him in forming a chamber orchestra. In August the Sisters of St. Mary celebrated their centenary in Texas (1873-1973) with a reception at Our Lady of Victory. The average Mass attendance for the month was 1,680. In September the St. Vincent de Paul Society appealed for donations for the victims of floods and earthquakes in Mexico. Joe Gapinski would pick up donated clothing and bedding. CCD classes began on Sunday, September 23, and the banns of marriage were announced for Dennis Crumley of St. Mary's and Malinda Rhodes of St. Patrick's Cathedral. This would be the fourth generation of his

CHAPTER 7

Glories Restored

family to be married at St. Patrick's, beginning with his maternal great-grandparents.

The greatest need of all when Monsignor Wiewell became pastor was the improvement of the St. Ignatius building. The basement area had been renovated earlier, but the three upper floors were in deplorable condition. Carole Weaver was conducting a CCD program there for about ninety students, but the building was not a fit place for educating children.

As it happened, Sister Bonaventure Mangan was in the process of supervising the renovation of the old Laneri High School building on Hemphill. It was to become a special learning center bearing Bishop Cassata's name. She was employing two extraordinarily skillful renovators from the firm of Jones and Hall. Wiewell was impressed with the project and invited the two to look at St. Ignatius with a view to doing something there. Carole Weaver drew up a floor plan for the three floors, designed to provide the best layout for the maximum number of classrooms and the necessary office space for an expanded program of religious education. Following her plan, the renovators did the work between May and October of 1974. It was a radical renovation, not merely a superficial one. Floors and walls were torn out and replaced. New electrical wiring and plumbing were installed. Restrooms were added and central heating put in. Not only the interior but also the exterior was done over. Doors opening onto porches that no longer existed were converted into windows. Planter boxes were added to provide exterior beauty, and dangerous steps were carpeted.

The end result was a beautiful building. The nineteenth century structure was given back some of the glory of its earlier days and made useful in twentieth century terms.

With the completion of the renovation the enrollment increased greatly. Each year new desks had to be purchased to seat the increased number of students. Monsignor Wiewell, in a recent interview, said that the drawing power of the school of religion was a significant factor in the growth of the parish during his pastorate.

Other things claimed the attention of the parish as well. The parking areas had to be repaved and new sidewalks poured. Planter boxes and hedges were added; old trees were removed. The front rooms of the rectory were panelled. The air-conditioning units in the rectory were replaced, and new copper cooling and heating pipes were put in throughout the system. The rectory was repainted inside and out (three times). The statues and the stations in the church were redone, and the statue of Our Lady of Guadalupe was placed in the sanctuary. The pews and the floors were repainted. The choir loft was renovated. A new organ was purchased and installed, as well as a synthesizer, kettle drums, and chimes. To top it off, the bells, which had not been heard for a long time, sounded again thanks to a timed, electronic striking system which was added.

The final project which Monsignor Wiewell contemplated was the enlargement of the sacristy. Through all the years of St. Patrick's history its clergy and people had endured a truly tiny sacristy, no more than 12 x 15 feet in size. The size of the room made vesting impossible there for anything other than a simple, one-priest Mass. For years, since the beginning, bishops and clergy had assembled in the front rooms of the rectory to vest for larger celebrations, diocesan functions, Holy Week services, and ordinations. In addition, storage space for vestments of priests and servers, as well as other items used in worship, was

Monsignor John M. Wiewell proudly inspects the foundations of the new addition to the cathedral.
Photo courtesy of The North Texas Catholic.

Monsignor Wiewell decided to correct all these problems. To begin with, he commissioned a study or survey of the building and its environs to be done. This project was entrusted to Dr. James Patrick, A.I.A., who researched the beginnings of the church and, with the meager resources available (for much important data had been lost or destroyed over the years) traced the history of the structure with all its features through the hundred years. The result of his work, "Survey of the Fabric of St. Patrick's," has been an invaluable resource for the preparation of this book.

Monsignor Wiewell ran into considerable opposition over his project. Controversy was, perhaps, inevitable given the antiquity of the church. St. Patrick's Cathedral is an important historical landmark building. Important historical landmarks should be preserved. They should not be added to nor substantially altered lest they lose their original character. Nothing should be added or taken away which would make the church different from what it was originally.

On the other hand, St. Patrick's is also an active and busy parish church used by hundreds every week. Twenty-five hundred people attending Sunday Mass, the many weddings and funerals, and the requirements of the regular diocesan functions, all seemed to point to the need for the new facility.

The purists argued their case persuasively. The needs, described by Monsignor Wiewell were admitted; but if a new sacristy were to be built, it should be detached from the church itself and stand alone. The Parish Council was the arena of the debate. The result was that, although the new facilities were to be built, and as a part of the church, it was to be done in such a way as to be virtually undetectable from the interior of the church and harmonious to the eye from the outside. The new addition and the old structure were to match.

The new sacristy, a very spacious one, along with the bride's room, restrooms, and ramp was completed in 1985. Stained glass windows were designed and ordered, and a magnificent bronze bas relief of St. Patrick, six feet in height, was affixed to the south exterior wall. It was sculpted by architectural artist Gordon Smith. The first window to be installed depicts the newly canonized St. Maximilian Kolbe. Another window honors Father Guyot. The new

severely limited by the size of the room. Many vestments and Mass items had to be kept in closets and vesting cases in the basement of the church. There was no easy access to that basement, either. It had always been a difficulty for the clergy, and especially for the sacristan.

There were other problems in the church which needed correction. There was no going in and out of the church without climbing steps. This was a matter of considerable difficulty for handicapped persons. New churches, all new public buildings in fact, prided themselves on being wheel chair accessible. Besides that, there was pressure from the fire department for another exit. They were concerned with safety. Other things, taken for granted in new churches, were lacking. Restroom facilities were one; space for wedding parties to prepare themselves to walk up the aisle was another.

construction also provides for access to the basement and the crypt chapel from within the building. The old basement entry with its sign, "Watch Thy Step," was sealed. It was a big job and an expensive one, costing in excess of $600,000, many times the cost of the original building one hundred years before. The new sacristy was dedicated by Bishop Delaney on April 13, 1986.

It was the last major project undertaken by Monsignor Wiewell before his retirement. The usual age for retirement of priests in the Diocese of Fort Worth is 75. Bishop Delaney kindly waived this rule so that Monsignor could celebrate the 50th anniversary of his ordination to the priesthood and his retirement as pastor simultaneously.

It was a point of satisfaction to Monsignor Wiewell that upon his retirement he left the parish debt free and with a substantial amount in savings despite the heavy cost of all these improvements, especially the sacristy project. The people of St. Patrick's, proud of their church, sustained their pastor in all his endeavors. Monsignor Wiewell is a frequent and welcome visitor at St. Patrick's.

Many priests served with Wiewell in those fourteen years. Fathers Reginald Kelly, Eugene Witkowski, Frank Carlin, and Thomas Taaffe were there at the outset. Fathers Frank Uroda,

Don and Frances Hopkins, sacristans for many years at St. Patrick's Cathedral. *Photo courtesy of Mr. and Mrs. Don Hopkins.*

Joseph Determan, O.P., Francis Zimmerer, O.S.B., Dennis Smith, and John Vega were assistants in the early days. Monsignor Raymond Garcia was at St. Patrick's for a while and administered San Mateo. Other assistants were Fathers Joseph Pemberton, John Hennessy, Christopher Davis, O.S.B., Charles Burns, and R. Dale Edwards. At the time of his retirement, the associates were Fathers Gary Geurtz and Gonzalo Morales. Father Dan Williams was in residence at one time, and Father Meinrad Marbaugh, O.S.B., often relieved in the summer months. Finally, everyone's job was made easier by the seven years of faithful Sunday help on the part of Father Michael McCarthy.

Monsignor Wiewell celebrated his Golden Jubilee as a priest in June 1987. Concelebrants were Father Gary Geurtz, right, and Father Gonzalo Morales, left. *Photo courtesy of St. Patrick Cathedral Archives.*

Associates and residents during the pastorate of Monsignor Wiewell: Row 1: (l. to r.) Father Frank Uroda, Father John Vega, Father Dennis Smith, Father Joseph Determan. Row 2: (l. to r.) Father Francis Zimmerer, Monsignor Ramón Garcia, Father Thomas Taaffe, Monsignor Charles King. Row 3: (l. to r.) Father Joseph Pemberton, Father John Hennessy, Father Chris Davis, O.S.B., Father Dale Edwards. Row 4: (l. to r.) Father John Donnelly, Father Dan Williams, Father Joseph Carlin, Father Meinrad Marbaugh, O.S.B. Row 5: (l. to r) Father Gary Geurtz, Father Gonzalo Morales.
Photos courtesy of The Texas Catholic *and* The North Texas Catholic.

CATHEDRA

The Catholic Encyclopedia contains the following information:
"Cathedral—the principal church of a diocese in which the bishop has his throne and where he preaches, teaches, and conducts religious services. The term is derived from the Greek word καθεδρα, which passed into Latin as *cathedra,* the word for the bishop's seat or throne. In the early Christian era the *cathedra* was a symbol of authority, and the expression *ex cathedra* signifies the solemn teaching authority of the pope as the successor of St. Peter. Although the bishop may set up a temporary throne within any church in his diocese, one particular edifice, usually in the city in which he resides, is designated for the establishment of a permanent *cathedra* and is called the diocesan cathedral. The original position of the bishop's chair was in the apse at the east end of the building, so that he looked westward across the high altar, at the congregation; but it is now customary to place it at the north (Gospel) side of the sanctuary. The usual throne is raised on three steps and surmounted by a canopy representative of the dignity of the episcopal office."

St. Patrick's Church attained the rank of co-cathedral on December 8, 1953, when the name of the Diocese of Dallas was changed to the Diocese of Dallas-Fort Worth. The honor was shared with Sacred Heart Cathedral in Dallas. This co-cathedral status lasted sixteen years until the founding of the Diocese of Fort Worth on August 22, 1969. The chair, the *cathedra,* was in use in St. Patrick's Church from the 1930's. It was sometimes employed as a temporary throne for Bishop Joseph P. Lynch of Dallas at important functions in the church. When the church became a co-cathedral, the chair was moved to the spot it

Bishop Joseph P. Lynch of Dallas.
Photo courtesy of St. Patrick Cathedral Archives.

presently occupies, and a temporary canopy was installed above it. Monsignor O'Donohoe announced plans to have a permanent episcopal throne in the sanctuary "of hand-carved dark oak." The dozel, or crown, above the episcopal throne was made in 1954 by N. Vidargas e Hijos, religious sculptors of Mexico City. The gold fringe and tassels of the draperies were made in France to Monsignor O'Donohoe's order. The existing chair continued to be used. Monsignor Wolf directed the refinishing and reupholstering of the chair as well as the rest of the sanctuary seating which matches the *cathedra.*

On October 21, 1969, Bishop John J. Cassata was led to the throne by the Apostolic Delegate, Archbishop Luigi Raimondi, and, seated there, received his crozier, another symbol of the authority of the first Bishop of Fort Worth.

On July 14, 1981, almost a year after Bishop Cassata's retirement, the Holy See announced the

Bishop Thomas K. Gorman of Dallas-Fort Worth.
Photo courtesy of St. Patrick Cathedral Archives.

Bishop John J. Cassata of Fort Worth led to the *cathedra* by the Apostolic Delegate, Archbishop Raimondi.
Photo courtesy of St. Patrick Cathedral Archives.

appointment of Father Joseph P. Delaney, a priest of the Diocese of Brownsville, as the second Bishop of Fort Worth. The Massachusetts-born bishop-elect came to Fort Worth the same day for a press conference in St. Patrick's Cathedral. There he publicly accepted the appointment, "relying totally on the grace and the sustaining presence of Our Lord, Jesus Christ."

A committee was quickly formed to plan the ordination and installation of the new shepherd. The ceremony was set for September 13, 1981. The Tarrant County Convention Center was chosen as the site in order to accommodate the large number of participants expected from all over the diocese and beyond its borders. The huge arena was appropriately arranged with a spacious stage. The *cathedra* was transported from St. Patrick's Cathedral and placed in the position of honor at the head of the large platform. There, in the presence of 9,000 people, Bishop Delaney was ordained to the order of bishop and formally led to the *cathedra* by Archbishop Patricio Flores of San Antonio, the principal ordainer.

The ordination ceremony paid tribute to the history of the area by having representatives of all the parishes enter in procession in the order in which the parishes were established. St. Patrick's, as the oldest, led the procession, followed by St. Mary's, Gainesville, St. Mary's, Henrietta, St. Stephen's, Weatherford . . . to the last parish to be established. The Litany of the Saints included the names of the titular patrons of all parishes in the diocese.

Opposite Page:

Ordination of Bishop Joseph P. Delaney on September 13, 1981, at the Tarrant County Convention Center.
Photo courtesy of **The Texas Catholic.**

Bishop Thomas K. Gorman kneels to receive the blessing of newly ordained Father Robert Wilson on May 27, 1957. This was the first recorded ordination in St. Patrick's Church. Father Robert Rehkemper and Father Carl Vogel are in the background.
Photo courtesy of Father Robert Wilson.

Father Ryenold Matus receives the Sign of Peace from Bishop John J. Cassata at his ordination in St. Patrick's, December 8, 1979. Father Ramón Durán and Father Dan Williams are on either side of the bishop.
Photo courtesy of Father Ryenold Matus.

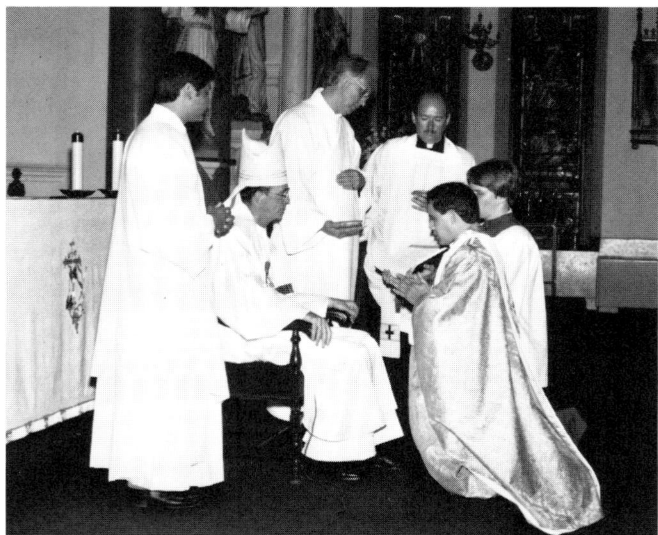

Bishop Delaney ordained Father Richard Flores to the priesthood on June 9, 1984. To the Bishop's right is Father Hector Medina ordained at St. Patrick's two weeks later. Flores and Medina are both native sons of St. Patrick's Cathedral parish.
Photo courtesy of St. Patrick Cathedral Archives.

Shortly before Monsignor Wiewell's retirement in June of 1987, a parish profile was drawn up at the request of the Diocesan Personnel Board. The information given in the profile provides a good outline for a word picture of St. Patrick's Parish and its people at the time of the one hundredth anniversary of the laying of the cornerstone.

The profile reports that there are 1,365 registered families comprising some 3,935 individuals. It estimates that there are 300 families or 750 people who at least participate and are not registered. Two percent of the parishioners are black. Thirty-eight percent of the families have Hispanic surnames. The average age of the parishioners was estimated to be 50 and above, but there are many younger individuals and young families. There are always many babies at Sunday Mass. An average of 120 babies are baptized each year. There is a large number of elderly people, many of them shut-in, and their spiritual care is an important part of the mission of the parish. Although a significant number of parishioners live within the parish boundaries, most do not. The census shows that registered parishioners come from all parts of Tarrant County and beyond. This is not surprising. It has always been so, throughout the parish's long history. Sunday Mass attendance averages 2,400. On Christmas and Easter almost twice that many attend.

The people of the Cathedral parish are proud of their church. Indeed, the beauty of the church is the reason many people join it. The people are also generous and supportive. In the year preceding the survey, contributions came to $450,000. The generosity of the people has made it possible not only to function as a parish but also to help other parishes and institutions in need. The generosity goes far beyond the pocketbook. The people cheerfully volunteer to help not only with continuing programs but also with special needs whenever these are made known to them.

The mission of the parish is supported by an active Parish Council of sixteen members. Some of the members are chosen by the parish at large in annual elections. Others are chosen as representatives of parish departments and organizations. Some hold office by appointment of the pastor. Presently serving on the Parish Council are Jim Barros, John Barton, Marion Burda, Pat Coyne, Malinda Crumley, Vincent

CHAPTER 8

The 100th Year

Fialho, Robert McAvoy, Ed Mikes, Carmen Rios, John Wilson, Norma Adkins, Dyane Atwood, Gerald Kramer, Ricki Migues, and David Schneider. Jim Barros is president. The Council operates according to a carefully drawn up constitution, the work of Vincent Fialho, based on diocesan guidelines.

The religious education department of the parish conducts its activities in the St. Ignatius building, except on Sunday morning, when the large number of children attending CCD classes requires that they use the lower level of the rectory as well. The entire department is under the direction of Mrs. Carole Weaver, D.R.E., who not only supervises the department but has actually built it up, step by step, program by program, since she began with almost nothing seventeen years ago. She is assisted by Mrs. Fran Davis, general secretary, Mrs. Barbara Sharp for sacramental preparation, Mr. Ed Lobb for RCIA, and Ms. Anna Bankhead for services to youth. The School of Religion relies on 45 teachers, auxiliaries, and hall supervisors, all of them willing volunteers. The percentage of certified teachers is very high, and continuing catechist formation is a high priority for the D.R.E. Mrs. Weaver inaugurated the RCIA two years ago with the help of Mrs. Cindy Brennan. Brother Ed Kiefer, S.M., co-ordinated the process in its second year, and Mr. Lobb is in charge as the RCIA moves into its third year. Sunday mornings are alive with religious education activities from early morning on. In the year of the survey, seventy-three children were prepared for First Communion, and twenty-six young people were confirmed. Thirty-one adults entered the Church through the RCIA process.

A formation board advises the D.R.E. about the programs. Members of the board are Mrs. Weaver, Robert McAvoy, John and Mary Wilson, Gerald Kramer, Barbara Sharp, and Sister Anna Lozano. Mr. McAvoy represents the board and the department on the Parish Council.

An important part of day-to-day parish life is the Social and Charitable Services Office. This office is operated by Deacon Joseph Raetz and is open four hours each day, six days a week. Deacon Raetz's department works in close cooperation with the St. Vincent de Paul Society under the chairmanship of Mr. Ed Mikes, who also represents this department on the Parish Council. The number of requests for help is large. In the second quarter of 1988 assistance was given to 663 persons, adults and children. A wide range of needs was met. The office provided 225 grocery orders and 78 food and lodging vouchers. It gave 267 bus tokens and 21 bus tickets for destinations outside Fort

Opposite Page:

The religious education department in 1988. Left to right: Ed Lobb, RCIA director; Fran Davis, department secretary; Anna Bankhead, youth ministry, and Carole Weaver, who has built the program from scratch since she began 17 years ago.
Photo courtesy of St. Patrick Cathedral/David Barros photographer.

Robert Theisen, Ed Mikes, Deacon Joe Raetz and Joe Gapinski are pictured at the entrance to Deacon Raetz's Social and Charitable Services office.
Photo courtesy of St. Patrick Cathedral/David Barros photographer.

Worth. Twenty-six people were helped with gasoline, twelve with pharmacy needs, three with rent, and one with utilities. Eighty-six visits were made, and 168 referrals were made to other agencies.

Clients of the office include families and individuals, some parishioners, most not. Deacon Raetz deals with a large number of homeless and unemployed people as well as with stranded travelers. The important thing is that Deacon Raetz receives each person with courtesy and patience. He is no pushover but would rather err by being generous than turn away someone in real need. The parishioners are happy to have this office acting in their name and willingly supply Deacon Raetz and the St. Vincent de Paul Society with the resources necessary for their work.

The St. Patrick's Fraternity of the St. Vincent de Paul Society was founded March 14, 1948. The charter members were Frank Greiner, A. E. Witkowski, Walter Klein,, Sr., Walter Klein, Jr., Frank Yeager, Frank Mills, Art H. Elshoff, Eugene F. Schenk, and J. V. Pyka. The current members are Ed Mikes, Joe Gapinski, Robert Theisen, Ken Humphreys, Joseph Unsworth, and Frank Crumley.

Inside the rectory are the parish offices, and here the key person is Mrs. Edith Hardwick.

Known to all the parishioners as "Edie," she is Executive Secretary and Business Manager of the parish. She handles everything from the parish bookkeeping to requests for Masses, to the sacramental registers, to filling the pamphlet racks. The priests and parishioners expect her to be able to handle anything that comes along, to answer any question, and to find any needed item at a moment's notice. Generally, she can do all these things. She has handled the job for almost nineteen years, working with three different pastors, always with the same efficiency and serenity. Edie's backup person is Mrs. Olivia Gutierrez, who takes charge of the office in vacation times and those days when the pressure of parish business is particularly heavy.

The post of Archivist and Historian belongs to Mrs. Kay Fialho. Her job also includes directing tours. The job was intended to be a part-time one, but in the summer of 1988 it became a double-time job instead. The parish archives are far from complete, and the task of assembling the necessary materials for a centennial book was a formidable one. Many brief histories of the parish have been written over the years, and the debt of this project to their authors is gratefully acknowledged. Yet, most of them were sketchy, and some relied on inaccurate

Elizabeth Ladkins offers refreshment to Edie Hardwick, executive secretary and business manager; Kay Fialho, archivist-historian, and Father William Hoover, pastor, as they look at some of the photographs to appear in this book. *Photo courtesy of St. Patrick Cathedral/David Barros photographer.*

information. Mrs. Fialho has gone back to the primary sources, spending hours by the hundreds scanning newspapers from the last century and the early part of this one, conducting interviews with people knowledgeable about the history of the parish, and checking out materials in other archival collections. She has made hundreds of phone calls, followed innumerable leads and hunches—some of them dead ends—and begging, borrowing, and cajoling to obtain the needed information. Putting together the collection of photographs which grace this volume was a major task in itself. Kay has a knack for what she does, and she enjoys it. Parish historians of the future will bless her.

Other rectory employees, seldom seen but much appreciated by the priests and the staff, are Mrs. Elizabeth Ladkins, Mrs. LaRue Green, Mrs. Lottie Parker, and Mrs. Agnes Owens. These ladies take excellent care of the rectory and the priests.

The senior member of the parish staff is Richard Valdez, who has been Director of Maintenance and Custodial Services for twenty-five years, one-fourth of the span of the church's history. Old buildings require not only much hard work but considerable understanding, and Mr. Valdez knows all the ins and outs of all three buildings. He came to St. Patrick's from Holy Name in 1963 and has dedicated himself since then to the maintenance, cleanliness, and beauty of the parish buildings and property. Parishioners and visitors alike notice and enjoy the carefully trimmed landscape and the seasonal flowers always in bloom. Few are aware, though, to what extent the parish facilities depend on the knowledge and skills of this one man. Richard is assisted in his task by Fredrick Valdez, his son, and, when the demands are heavy, by Anthony Valdez, another son. They are quite a team, and St. Patrick's is fortunate to have them.

Inside the church a great many people are responsible for the beauty and dignity of the worship. Music is of the utmost importance, and James Barros has been in charge of music at St. Patrick's for twenty-one years as choirmaster, organist, and music director. He is seconded by Miss Karen McNeill, assistant organist, and a choir whose roots go back more than 100 years. The choir is featured in another section of this book.

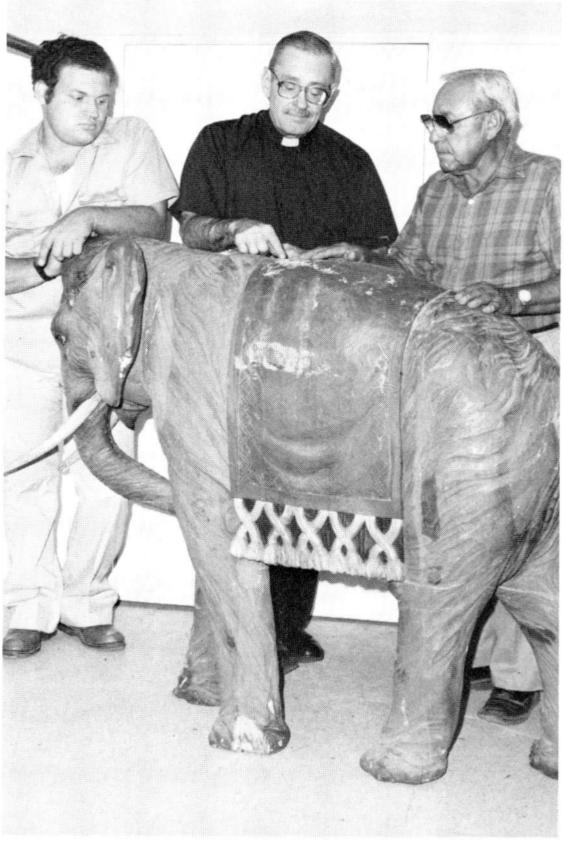

The Christmas elephant has been an attraction at St. Patrick's for many years. Anthony Valdez (left), Father Hoover, and Richard Valdez, director of maintenance and custodial services, plan some needed repairs on the 40-year-old bearer of the Magi. *Photo courtesy of St. Patrick Cathedral/David Barros photographer.*

Frederick Valdez, assistant custodian, shows the basement entrance as it used to be. *Photo courtesy of St. Patrick Cathedral Archives.*

James Barros, organist-choirmaster, and Karen McNeill, assistant, go over their plans for a Sunday liturgy.
Photo courtesy of St. Patrick Cathedral/David Barros photographer.

Baldwin Stanton and Nunia Roik share a pleasant moment in the new sacristy. Mrs. Roik is sacristan of St. Patrick's Cathedral. Stanton has rendered faithful service to the Cathedral for more than four decades.
Photo courtesy of St. Patrick Cathedral/David Barros photographer.

A trained and dedicated corps of acolytes, ushers, lectors, extraordinary Eucharistic ministers, and altar boys numbering more than 100 persons carry out the necessary ministerial functions at Sunday and Holy Day Masses. These ministers serve under the direction of David Yaniko, Eucharistic ministers chairman; William McDanel, chairman of lectors; and John Flynn, captain of the ushers.

Acolytes designate are present at each Mass to assist the celebrant and to direct the movements of the other ministers in the sanctuary. The captain of this group is Jon Drew Hartmann. Present members of the team of acolytes are Robert Simmons, Cecil Laizure III, Ron Mueller, Ron Roik, Hubert Andrews, Tom Lane, Joseph Meyers, Ernest West, Alan Alpar, and Joseph Olsen. Gerald Kramer is in charge of altar boy training.

Of great importance to the liturgy are also those who assist the priest at the weekday Masses. They are: Robert Simmons, Patrick O'Neil, Joe DeGrazier, Randy Meyers, John Tharp, Tom Lane, and, most worthy of mention, Baldwin Stanton, who has served the church and the sanctuary with great fidelity for half a century.

The post of sacristan has always been an important one at St. Patrick's. Following in the footsteps of Margaret Lehane, Martin Baskin, Nedege Turley, and Don and Frances Hopkins, is Mrs. Nunia Roik. Mrs. Roik sees to the appointments of the church and sacristy, preparations for Mass, and decoration of the church for Sundays, feast days, and special occasions. She also assists wedding parties in their preparations and directs the flow of each marriage ceremony. A quiet smile, a gentle word, and a sharing of years of experience are what she offers the sometime nervous bride and groom and others involved in special ceremonies. Others might panic, but Nunia— never! She is responsible for much of the beauty and dignity for which services at St. Patrick's are noted.

A recent addition to the ministries of the parish is the corps of hospital and shut-in visitors who bring Holy Communion and what help and comfort they can provide to the ill and the disabled. Established by Father Gonzalo Morales in the summer of 1987, this group is headed by Ron Roik, chairman, and Dyane Atwood, co-chairman. The visitors are Nancy

San Mateo Catholic Church, sister parish of St. Patrick's Cathedral. *Photo courtesy of St. Patrick Cathedral/David Barros photographer.*

Murphy, Francine Reynolds, Ever Horan, Anna Williams, Rudy Dolkos, Sylvia Dolkos, Baldwin Stanton, and Charles Thomason. Other members of the team are Helen Pryor, Drew Hartmann, Berlu Cabral, Bob Kelly, and Maria Reyna.

Since St. Patrick's is the cathedral of the diocese, the bishop is frequently the officiant in the sanctuary. The parish is always happy to be host to diocesan functions. The Cathedral belongs to the whole local church, and everyone should feel at home there.

Also necessary to the smooth functioning of the church is the work of the Altar Society. This group provides hosts and wine, altar candles and vestments, and prepares the church for Sunday Mass. Ricki Migues is president of the society, assisted by three vice-presidents, Nancy Mills, Imelda Peschel, and Rose Flores. Nancy Murphy is secretary, Olivia Gutierrez, treasurer, and June Stewart, parliamentarian.

The Missionary Catechists of the Sacred Hearts of Jesus and Mary, usually called the "Madres Violetas," are an important part of the life of the parish. Brought to Fort Worth in 1960 by Father Hoover, they have conducted the catechetical programs at San Mateo and at the Santo Niño center on Grant Street ever since. In 1987 Bishop Delaney appointed Sister Guadalupe Aleman and Sister Anna Lozano as pastoral administrators of San Mateo Parish. The sisters are also involved in the Sunday morning school of religion at St. Patrick's.

Sister Anna Maria Lozano and Sister Guadalupe Aleman, members of the Missionary Catechist Sisters of the Sacred Hearts of Jesus and Mary, are pastoral administrators of San Mateo Parish. The two sisters are also active in the St. Patrick's School of Religion at its St. Ignatius and Grant Street campuses.

Berlu and Mary Cabral at the gate of the Santo Niño Center on Grant Street. The Cabrals take care of the property, which is near their home.
Photo courtesy of St. Patrick Cathedral/David Barros photographer.

Mention needs to be made of Toni Cruz, Sunday evening sacristan, and Berlu Cabral, who cares for the Grant Street Center. They, too, are part of the team that makes St. Patrick's an effective parish.

Of course, there were a host of others over the 100 years whose service to their parish was invaluable and whom we recall with gratitude. Many thousands of Fort Worth Catholics have worshipped God in St. Patrick's, received Communion, confessed their sins, and made the church a part of their spiritual journey. Their number cannot be counted. There are, however, two numbers that can be given here which tell us something of the 100 years of service. On July 17, 1988, the total number of baptisms reached 18,428, and on July 30, 1988, Ramon Carrillo and Lori Gattis were the 2,966th couple to be married at St. Patrick's.

The present pastor, Father William Hoover, came to St. Patrick's on June 17, 1987. His sole notable achievement is the volume you hold in your hands. He hopes it will be an inspiration to you and your children. For himself—he hopes to make it big in the book of the second century.

Father Michael McCarthy
Photo courtesy of The North Texas Catholic.

Father James Hanlon
Photo courtesy of The North Texas Catholic.

Father Salvador Perez
Photo courtesy of St. Patrick Cathedral/David Barros photographer.

Father Thomas Teczar.
Photo courtesy of St. Patrick Cathedral/David Barros photographer.

SELECTED BIBLIOGRAPHY

BOOKS

Castaneda, Carlos E. *Our Catholic Heritage in Texas*. Ed. Carlos E. Cortes et al. Reprinted. Vol VII. New York: Arno, 1976. 1-561.

Comaskey, B. J. "Cathedral." New Catholic Encyclopedia. 1967 ed.

Corcoran, Sister Mary Louise. *Seal of Simplicity: A Life of Mother Emilie*. Westminister, Maryland: Newman Press, 1958.

The Shamrock. Laneri High School Yearbook, 1925. Fort Worth: Booker Printing & Book Co., Inc., 1925.

Wewers, Damian. *St. Mary of the Assumption Catholic Church*. Ed. Dr. Catherine Kenney Carlton and Madeline Crimmins Williams. Fort Worth: 1968.

Williams, Mack. *In Old Fort Worth*. Ed. Madeline Williams et al. Fort Worth: The News Tribune, 1977.

NEWSPAPER ARTICLES

"Churches." *Fort Worth Standard* 27 May 1875.

"The Festival Last Night." *Fort Worth Daily Democrat* 22 Sept. 1876.

"The First High Mass Ever Celebrated in Fort Worth by the Roman Catholic Church." *Fort Worth Daily Standard* 30 Oct. 1876.

"Strawberry Festival." *Fort Worth Daily Democrat* 21 May 1877.

"Church Chimes." *Fort Worth Daily Democrat* 16 Feb. 1879.

"Church Chimes." *Fort Worth Daily Democrat* 23 Feb. 1879.

"Aid for the Afflicted." *Fort Worth Daily Democrat* 9 Sept. 1879.

"More Funds for the Fever Districts." *Fort Worth Daily Democrat* 12 Sept. 1879.

"Church Chimes." *Fort Worth Daily Democrat* 30 Nov. 1879.

"Churches." *Fort Worth Daily Democrat* 10 Dec. 1879.

"The Catholic Supper." *Fort Worth Daily Democrat* 18 Dec. 1879.

"Churches." *Fort Worth Daily Democrat* 20 Dec. 1879.

"New Catholic Church." *Fort Worth Daily Gazette* 15 Oct. 1888.

"The Dedication." *Fort Worth Gazette* 10 July 1892.

"The Life of Father Guyot Linked with Catholic Progress Here." *Fort Worth Telegram* 4 Aug. 1907.

"A Good Man Is Dead." *Fort Worth Telegram* 4 Aug. 1907.

"Father Guyot Dies after Long Illness." *Fort Worth Record* 4 Aug. 1907.

"Tears Flow at Service." *Fort Worth Telegram* 6 Aug. 1907.

"Great Pipe Organ Will Play July 10" *Fort Worth Record* 9 July 1913.

"St. Patrick's Event Draws Great Crowd." *Fort Worth Star Telegram* 11 July 1913.

"Silver Jubilee to Be Observed." *Fort Worth Star Telegram* 5 June 1923.

"Masked Parade Staged Here by Klan Women Viewed by Thousands." *Fort Worth Star Telegram* 9 June 1923.

"Breaking Ground at St. Mary's Church." *Fort Worth Star Telegram* 28 Nov. 1923.

"Father J. G. O'Donohoe Pleads for the Return of Liturgical Color." *Southern Messenger* [Dallas and Houston, Tx] 24 Feb. 1927.

"Three Religions, One Faith in America." *Fort Worth Press* 23 May 1929.

"Catholics, Non-Catholics Pay Tribute as Funeral for Msgr. Nolan Is Arranged." *Fort Worth Star Telegram* 26 Dec. 1929.

"Clergymen from 3 States to Assist at Nolan Burial." *Fort Worth Star Telegram* 27 Dec. 1929.

"Service to Be in New Scene." *Fort Worth Star Telegram* 8 July 1934.

"Priest in Rome for Two Years to Study Law." *Fort Worth Star Telegram* 5 Oct. 1953.

"Msgr. Vincent Wolf, Now at Dallas, Named St. Patrick's Cathedral Pastor." *Fort Worth Star Telegram* 3 Mar. 1956.

"Pastor and Steering Committee Meet on St. Patrick's Restoration Drive." *Fort Worth Star Telegram* 5 June 1956.

"St. Patrick Co-Cathedral Restoration Fund Drive Undertaken by Parishioners to Raise $150,000." *The Texas Catholic* 11 June 1956.

"Little Mary, First in Line When School Opened Here in 1885, Goes Back at 79." *Fort Worth Press* 17 June 1956.

"Radio Speaker." *Fort Worth Star Telegram* 1 Dec. 1956.

"New Pastor of St. Patrick's 'Back Home' after 19 Years." *Fort Worth Star Telegram* 21 Jan. 1962.

"Monsignor DeFalco Elevated to Bishopric." *Fort Worth Star Telegram* 17 April 1963.

"Turnstile." *Amarillo Globe-Times* 23 Oct. 1963.

"Co-Cathedral Sets Burning of Note." *Fort Worth Star Telegram* 3 Feb. 1968.

"Rites in Dallas and Fort Worth Welcome Bishop John J. Cassata." *The Texas Catholic* 29 June 1968.

"Requiem Mass Set for Church Rector." *Fort Worth Press* 5 Feb. 1973.

"Open House Set for Renovated St. Ignatius Building." *The Texas Catholic* 31 Oct. 1975.

"Bishop Lawrence DeFalco, Former Pastor in FW, Dies." *Fort Worth Star Telegram* 23 Sept. 1979.

INTERVIEWS 1985—1988

Barros, Jim
Becan, Al
Becan, Robert
Bransford, Mary
Breedlove, Father Larry
Coleman, Dr. Thomas
Cowan, Dorothy
Davidson, Polly
Duross, Vincent
Eitleman, E. F.
Fenelon, Margaret
Fenelon, Anna
Gordon, Gayle
Gilchrist, W. R.
Griffin, Lucy
Hardwick, Edith
Hazel, Patrick
Hopkins, Frances
Lehane, Dorothy
Manning, Herb
Noah, Jim
Paez, Jesús
Pritchett, Susan
Schmidt, Ruby
Simons, Lillian
Sister Bridget Mary
Thompson, Guy
Wiewell, Msgr. John
Wolf, Msgr. Vincent
Womack, Margaret
Xuereb, Father Publius

MANUSCRIPTS, LETTERS, AND ARCHIVAL MATERIAL

Carrico, Rose. Letter to Msgr. Joseph G. O'Donohoe, September 15, 1940. St. Patrick Cathedral Archives, Fort Worth.

Coggeshall, Linda. Narrative written for application to State for historical marker status, 1978. Tarrant County Junior College Northeast Campus History Department, Fort Worth.

Davis, Sister Teresa Ann. "The Development of Catholic Education in the Diocese of Dallas, Texas 1869-1949." Master's Thesis. 1950. Catholic University of America, Washington.

Fort Worth Chamber of Commerce. "Fort Worth." June, 1949. St. Patrick Cathedral Archives, Fort Worth.

"The Fort Worth National Bank Century One: 1873-1973." St. Patrick Cathedral Archives, Fort Worth.

Gunkle, Georgia Colvin. "St. Ignatius Academy, 1906-1909." Autobiographical narrative. St. Patrick Cathedral Archives, Fort Worth.

Hoffmeyer, Michael C. "Fort Worth Architecture, A History and Guide, 1873-1933." Master's Thesis. 1980. The University of Texas at Arlington.

Minutes, Trustee Regular Meetings, Incorporation of St. Ignatius Academy, 1885-1910. Tarrant County Historical Archives, Fort Worth.

Notes from St. Ignatius diaries, 1888-1907. St. Patrick Cathedral Archives, Fort Worth.

Patrick, Dr. James, A.I.A. "Survey of the Fabric of St. Patrick's Cathedral." 1985. St. Patrick Cathedral Archives, Fort Worth.

CITY RECORDS

City Directories 1877-1910. Fort Worth Public Library.

COUNTY RECORDS

Deed Records of Tarrant County
Volume C, page 398
Volume R, page 259
Volume T, page 408
Volume T, page 409
Volume 34, page 185
Volume 36, page 402
Volume 37, page 87
Volume 37, page 88
Volume 37, page 439
Volume 40, page 489
Volume 40, page 490
Volume 42, page 523
Volume 48, page 234
Volume 50, page 243
Volume 52, page 10
Volume 55, page 62
Volume 55, page 620
Volume 79, page 356
Volume 103, page 619
Volume 129, page 497
Volume 936, page 214
Volume 938, page 175
Volume 3048, page 57.

ACKNOWLEDGEMENTS

The author gratefully acknowledges the contributions of others, without whose help this volume would not have been possible: Malinda Crumley for correcting and readying the text for printing, Vincent Fialho for researching the acquisition of the property of the church, Ruby Schmidt for help with research and pictures, and David Barros for taking the contemporary photographs and adapting those from the past.

Susie Pritchett researched and wrote the feature on St. Ignatius School. Margaret Womack prepared the article on the Cathedral Chorale and the Cathedral Classics Seminars, and Kevin Levy wrote the article on the St. Patrick's choir. The St. Patrick's parish council rendered assistance with the promotion and marketing of the book.

Thanks, too, to those who were interviewed about their recollections of earlier days and those who lent precious mementos and cherished photographs from the past.

St. Patrick's is also indebted to Joe Jara/Motheral Printing, to Type Case Inc., to Barron Litho Plate Company, and to LeWay Composing for their kind contributions.

Finally, Kay Fialho, St. Patrick's archivist/historian, put all the pieces together, and this book is the result.

INDEX